the CHIEF'S SON

Dear Hank and Diane,
We love you and Thank you
for helping to make our India
trip possible. Just a little
more of our beloved India!
Yours in Jesus,
Allen and Leoda
July 1989

the CHIEF'S SON

LEODA BUCKWALTER

Evangel
Press
301 N. Elm St.
Nappanee, Indiana 46550

Cover design: Tracey Owen

Library of Congress Catalog Card Number: 89-84625
ISBN: 0-916035-32-8

PHOTOTYPESET ◆ FOR QUALITY

Printed in the United States of America

3 2 1

To
Eric
because you encouraged me

Contents

Preface

It is my privilege to welcome you to an unforgettable spiritual experience—an unfolding picture of the irresistible reality of Christ building his church in northern India.

In *The Chief's Son* you will find *obedience* to our Lord's commission, *vision* for reaching the unreached, *compassion* for the lost, *faith* in the God of miracles, *praise* in the midst of despair, and *triumph* when defeat seemed certain.

This is the story of people in a close-knit tribal setting, held in bondage by the satanic forces of darkness, who are exposed to the light of the gospel. Their response is a joy to behold.

The chief's son, Pradhan, is the one whom that light focused with intensity. Evangelist Benjamin's word to Pradhan is clear, "The price of following Jesus is high, but he's worth it." But the tribal leaders, including his father—the old chief, refused to have a Christian as chief. A true-to-life struggle ensued. Pradhan had to make a choice: to follow Christ, or become chief.

The Chief's Son is a beautiful illustration of God at work through the nitty-gritty of rejection, heartbreak, and suffering. I was captivated. I believe you will be also.

But this book has a special meaning for me. You see, I was privileged to be in Khanua the day Pradhan was baptized. The village was electrified with excitement. The chief's son had taken his stand as a confessing Christian.

Pradhan's story reminds us that missions pay great dividends. Faithful brothers and sisters responded to the call of our Lord to "Go into all the world." As a result, the Santal church in North India thrives under the blessing of God. In today's terminology, it is a "people group" reached and now reaching out to others of similar cultural background.

Praise the Lord for his love and faithfulness.

Samuel Wolgemuth
President Emeritus
Youth For Christ International

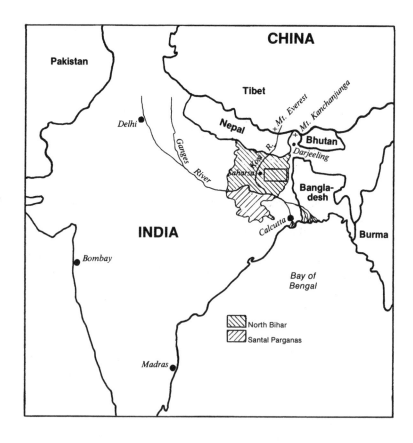

Map of Banmankhi Mission Area

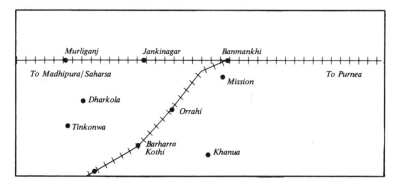

Introduction: Who Are the Santals?

The white-haired, brown-faced traveler stopped for a moment on his climb up Lokhonpur Mountain in Santal Parganas, India. He mopped his brow, sat in the shade of a sturdy *matkon* tree, and noted its wealth of red flowers, used by Santal housewives in their preparation of tasty curries.

The traveler, himself a Santal, stopped a moment to muse before continuing his journey. He had passed several villages on his route. None of the houses fronted the lanes, as do the homes of Hindus and Muslims. Instead, blank walls suggested that his people, the Santals, seek privacy—the right to live their own lives in their own way, using the language and tribal customs that have been theirs through the centuries.

The traveler smiled, and it was like a sunburst on his round face. Yes, we're different, he thought. We're Santals.

How different?

Practically all the inhabitants of North India come of Aryan stock, but the Santals, though living among them, are tribals of unknown origin, from without India. Instead of Aryan features, they have high cheekbones and flared nostrils, but not kinky hair, as do tribals in South India. Nor are they black in color, but range through light brown to dark brown.

Santals don't have temples, neither do they worship idols. Theirs is a religion of appeasement, wherein they strive to placate evil spirits called *bongas*. These serve under the command of their master, Satan.

Yet their traditions say they first worshiped the Great Spirit, Creator of heaven and earth. In Santali his name is Thakur Jiu.

Ask a Santal who he is, and he'll tell you "*hor hopon*," the true "son of man." All others are "troublemakers!" Not that he despises other races; he feels they are simply unfortunate. So he takes great pride in his heritage.

Tradition says the Santals migrated into India at least two thousand years ago, although there are no written records. Their well-developed sense of community helps to solidify the three to four million Santals who live in their homeland south of the Ganges River in Bihar. Others have moved eastward to Assam, and some have moved northward into Nepal. But they retain their Santal culture and forte of clearing jungles and planting grains. Nowadays, many work on tea plantations in the hills of Assam, and many there have turned to Christianity through the efforts of the Santal Mission (Lutheran).

Santal Parganas is a hilly country of about 4800 square miles, nearly as large as the state of Connecticut. Few roads challenge its privacy; trains skirt its borders. People travel by bus, oxcart, and mostly by foot.

The language, Santali, contrasts greatly with other Indian languages in that it is agglutinative. This means the student is given a root form, and the tools with which to build. There are twenty-seven verb tenses in Santali! A person can say exactly what he means—if he conquers those tenses! It's like building a house, with all the supplies laid in front of you, and you're told to put it together!

The language bears little or no resemblance to Hindi, except for borrowing some of the vocabulary because the Santals lived among Hindus and Muslims for centuries. But Santals cling to their own traditions. Though mingling in the marketplace, they come home to live in their own world, apart from other worlds.

Outwardly they are a happy people with a well developed sense of humor. They laugh easily, both at themselves and others. But the discerning begin to hear minor chords vibrate, chords of sadness, disappointment, and longing for freedom from bondage. Fear plays a dominant part in their lives, especially in their religion, and when they turn to Christ, they know inexplicable joy.

In some ways, the Santal woman is liberated, for she knows no *purdah*, as do Hindu and Muslim women. She moves freely, but usually with her own sex. In the long twilight hours, men seek one another's company, and women talk with women. In public meetings men sit in the foreground; women sit or stand in the back. One concludes that despite appearances, it still is a man's religion, and a man's land.

Yet Christianity has produced much change among Santals. How much, the traveler whom we first mentioned, knew.

He was a witch doctor, even leading other witch doctors with his prowess and magic skills. Secret potions, recited *mantras*, exorcism of demons—all this and more comprised his days and nights for much of his adult life in Santal Parganas. He beat the drums, an expert in all the rhythms. He sacrificed thousands of chickens, tearing them apart in the darkness with his bare hands and preparing them for the pot. Yet his expertise and his knowledge of witchcraft failed to give him peace of heart.

When Benjamin Marandi reached his mid-forties, he found himself baffled by a strange malady in his body. Neither his skill nor worshiping Hindu gods cleared it. After seeking deliverance for years, he met an English missionary who told him of Jesus.

At the witch doctor's request the white man came to his home and prayed a simple prayer of faith: "Let peace descend upon this house and all in it from this time forth, in the name of Jesus Christ, the Son of God."

It was enough!

The malady disappeared, never to return, and the witch doctor bowed to Jesus as victor over Satan and all his kin. That took place on a Tuesday. Sunday saw the former witch doctor in church, asking for baptism.

His subsequent years proved a song of devotion to the Lord who won him. Benjamin Marandi began to walk the hills and valleys that he surveyed from the summit of Lokhonpur Mountain. With the violin that now replaced his former drums, he sought to bring his people to Jesus, and his name and fame spread throughout the land.

In 1947 the Lord called him north of the river Ganges. He answered immediately, not hesitating as people are prone to do. For over thirty years, until the Lord called him home in 1979, this man of God sought those "other sheep" who were not yet in the fold of the Good Shepherd. When he died, his body was buried in the compound of a brick church near Purnea, among his people in North Bihar.

The Chief's Son records that venture. It focuses not on Santal Parganas, but on Khanua, a Santal village in North Bihar where it all started.

Benjamin, Dina, Pradhan, Dulu (name changed to make it easier to read), and Jatha are all actual people. Khanua's story needs to be told, a story that gives us the privilege of walking sandy trails with those who no longer live in darkness, but who now lead their own people to the Light.

Glossary

Benjamin—a converted Santal witch doctor who became an
evangelist to his people

Bhima—Lukhi's husband [pronounced **Bee**-*ma*]

bonga—an evil spirit, operating under Marang Buru (see below)
[***bone***-*ga*]

dikku—any non-Santal person; literally meaning "one who
makes trouble" [*dick-ku*]

Dina—the shortened name of Bellamdina, Benjamin's daughter;
used by everyone except her parents [***Dee***-*na*]

Dulu—Pradhan's uncle, only five years older than the chief's son

Gopal Singh—the landlord whose fields the Santals farmed as
share croppers; literally, Singh means "lion" in Hindi [***Go***-*puhl Sing*]

Jan-Guru—the leader of the witch doctors among the Santals
[*Jahn-**Guru***]

Khanua—a village in northern India [***Kuh***-*noo-ah*]

Lukhi—the wife of Bhima (one of the villagers); tortured as a
witch, she later became a Christian and took the name
Martha [***Loo***-*key*]

Manjli—literally means "middle one"; used as a proper name for
girls [*Muhn-jlee*]

Marang Buru—"Big Mountain"; the name Santals use for Satan
[*Muh-**rung** Boo-Roo*]

Pakku—means "little one"; used in endearment to refer to any
young girl, or as a proper name for the youngest daughter
[***Puh***-*kooh*]

pan—a digestive aid often taken after meals; made of betel nut
leaves; when chewed, the juice is red, like blood [*pahn*]

Pradhan—literally "leader" or "highest one"; the name of the
chief's son [*Pruh-**dahn***]

Raghu—chief of the village of Khanua [**Rah**-*ghoo*]

Ram Das—the landlord's son; literally "servant of Ram" (a Hindu god) [*Rahm-Dahs*]

Salku—Pradhan's brother; Raghu's second son [**Sahl**-*kooh*]

Santal—a tribal group living mainly in Santal Parganas, Bihar, India (see map) [*Sun-**tahl***]

Chapter One

The Hunters

At about four o'clock on an early October morning in 1941, two young men stole forth from adjacent courtyards in the Santal village of Khanua, North Bihar, India. Each carried a bow and poisoned arrows.

Dulu, the elder, aged twenty-two, greeted his companion, Pradhan, with a quiet smile. The willowy seventeen-year-old looked tense, his patrician features somber, but his eyes lit when he met his friend.

The teenager threw a green-checked cotton shawl around his otherwise bare shoulders. He stopped to secure his *dhoti* for easy running. This long white cloth, worn by the men as "pants," was now tied to ensure freedom of movement.

Dulu stood almost as tall as the chief's son, but had a heavier build. Of kindly features and ready smile, he now whispered, "Buddy, you can do it! I know you can! You'll bring in another wild boar today."

"If I don't," the boy muttered, "there's no wedding for me this year, and Manu lands my place on the village council."

"I saw him claim credit for the last boar you hit!"

"He's clever. He'll follow us now."

"No!" Pradhan's young uncle swung around and looked the boy in the face as he said earnestly, "I made sure my brother sends your cousin to Purnea today on important business. Don't fear! Manu's cultivating the chief, you know." He chuckled.

The two padded silently through the sleeping village, their bare feet throwing little puffs of dust as they ran the length of the lane between adobe houses. In villages other than those in which Santals lived, residences opened onto the roads, but among this tribal group, only bare whitewashed walls with no windows met

1

the eye. One had to probe deeper to find the heart of village life, for each house represented an extended family that lived in three or four buildings fronting an open courtyard, all facing inward.

Yet the Santals were a gregarious and animated people, who enjoyed a well developed sense of community. To encourage this, each house provided a ledge adaptable for sitting, some two feet off the ground, eighteen inches in width. It was part of a base that helped strengthen the entire structure, and ran around three sides. The fourth opened into the courtyard.

In this early morning hour, with yet no hint of dawn, the hunters carefully picked their way over narrow trails set midst low-lying rice fields beyond the village. In turn these led to well marked paths through mustard fields, and the pungent smell caused them to inhale deeply. The soft cooing of the doves in the flowering *matkon* trees speeded their steps, for Pradhan and Dulu knew that dawn would soon break. The river jungle still lay three miles distant. It bore promise of easy targeting when the big game would come to the river to drink.

Several hours later two triumphant young men returned from the hunt. They carried a wild boar of magnificent proportions, its legs tied together and slung on a pole. Enthusiastic shouts from both men and women welcomed the hunters as they passed the threshing floor outside Khanua village. Everyone knew there would be a feast tonight.

Raghu, Pradhan's father and the chief over this village of about five hundred, looked up from his rope-making as the two entered the courtyard. "So that's where you were, son! I wondered what happened to you."

The teenager wiped his perspiring brow, and the hunters laid their superb trophy on the ground. "I had to do it, Dad," Pradhan replied, "but it wouldn't have happened without Dulu."

"Nonsense!" his young uncle exclaimed. He touched his companion's shoulder lightly and his eyes shone as he commented, "Raghu, you've got a prince of a son! I'm proud of him. He's a dead shot, you know."

"Then why did he miss the last one?"

"He didn't. Pradhan felled that boar, not Manu."

"You lie!"

"I don't . . . and others attest to the same."

"But Manu . . ."

"We know Manu and his clever ways. He's angling for that seat on the village council at his cousin's expense. Just because he happens to be two years older doesn't mean that he should usurp your son's rightful position, Raghu."

"Manu has a different story," the chief muttered, yet his crafty eyes searched the faces of the two young men before him.

His eldest son drew himself to full height, then said, "Dad, all I ask is that you question not only Manu but some of the others. If you want to know my hunting abilities, why not come out with me like Dulu does?"

The chief shifted on his mat, then replied, "This infernal hip! Ever since I fell, it's been bothering. No, my hunting days are over. I used to lead, but no more. Son, I've hoped desperately that you would take my place. Perhaps that's why I almost fear to believe your uncle's report."

"Investigate for yourself, Dad. Ask the others. They're always watching me."

In village India, authority lies in the hands of the village council over whom the chief, or *manjhi*, holds complete sway. Though an autonomous body, the village identifies with others of like ethnic background and culture, and the sense of "community" remains strong. So Hindus, Muslims, and tribals all mingle freely in the marketplace, yet remain worlds apart. Each operates as a world within a world, maintaining different languages, religion, and social practices.

Raghu's queries concerning the killing of the boar proved Dulu to be right, and Manu the culprit. The elders liked Pradhan's courage when on the hunt, even though he was shy at home. He worked hard in the fields, and the villagers felt this to be important since they lived by sharecropping Gopal Singh's extensive lands. Their future chief should have not only authority, but a true empathy of spirit.

Kailash, a seasoned farmer and brave hunter, expressed himself to Raghu. As the chief and he sat on the mat under a mango tree, Kailash remarked, "I admire Pradhan, sir. He's just seventeen, but already he shows fine character traits."

"Like what?" the chief asked tersely.

"The way he took Manu's manipulations."

Raghu swung around and looked his companion full in the face. "What do you know about Manu?" he demanded.

"I was there, my friend. Your son shot that boar, but your nephew came in and claimed the honor. Said it was his arrow that felled the animal."

"You're sure of that?"

"Yes, sir . . . I saw it! If Manu had done that to me, I would have fought him."

"And Pradhan didn't?"

Kailash hand-rolled some tobacco in his palms, then making a cigarette, lit it and began to smoke. The chief watched him closely, then spit a long stream of tobacco onto the dusty road. Kailash said, "No, sir, he just went out and bagged a better one."

"You call that courage? Why didn't Pradhan face him outright?" he challenged.

"Manu's got the advantage in age, sir, and perhaps in brawn. But neither of those qualities impress me when I see your son's discipline of spirit. And sir, he knows timing. That's important! I don't think he's done with Manu yet."

"Hmmm . . . " the chief said with a thoughtful grunt.

Manu, only son of Raghu's elder brother, Guru, reported to the chief on his return from the District Headquarters. But to his dismay he found that Pradhan had triumphed during his absence. The swarthy, dark complexioned young man sought his uncle's ear only to be met with, "Why did you lie to me, Manu?"

"What do you mean, sir?" the young man asked. "I always tell the truth."

"Oh? So it's your word against all others? I've made inquiry and have come to my own conclusions."

Manu couldn't face that unflinching gaze. He shifted from one foot to the other as he stood before the chief. Raghu, seated on the verandah, continued, "You've done many clever things, young man, but this time you've gone too far. My people tell me that Pradhan shot that boar, not you!"

"It's a conspiracy!" the young man cried. "They wait until I'm gone and then make up their stories."

"Hold!" the chief demanded sternly. "I'm not done with you yet. I have more to say. You are seeking power for yourself. In our Santal community, nobody seeks power at the expense of another," the chief warned. "You have done so, belittling my son, falsifying his accomplishments to me, and seeking the position of next-of-kin to the chief."

"It's a lie! It's a lie!"

"That's the way a *dikku* acts, Manu, and among them you will go. I banish you from this village for three months."

"Gladly, sir. The *dikkus* (a term literally meaning trouble-makers, used of all non-Santals by Santals) will welcome me."

"Go! You return only on good behavior."

Manu bowed low, and left. But bitterness raged within his spirit, and he vowed he would yet conquer.

Khanua village had never experienced a wedding like that which the chief gave his son, Pradhan. It came at the end of the harvest season, with everyone invited to the wedding feast that lasted three days and nights. Plenty of rice beer made the long evenings pleasant for the men who gathered in the chief's court-yard to spin tales while the women prepared the meal. They sat on their haunches in a large circle, cotton sheets drawn around their shoulders to give a degree of warmth from the evening chill. In the center, a bonfire leaped upward cheerfully and added a festive touch to the occasion.

Five adobe houses with thatched roofs surrounded the well-swept courtyard. Raghu's was the most commodious, sheltering himself and his family of four sons. Guru, Manu's father, and elder brother to the chief, lived in another. Raghu used the third for storing grains and produce. A fourth sheltered his animals. Pradhan and Manjli's new home, the last constructed, sat adjacent to Raghu's, even as his eldest son would now take his place next to the chief on all occasions.

Off to one side, near the entrance from the road, the *manjhi-than* proclaimed Raghu's status. An open shed used for council meetings, its mud platform stood a foot above the rest of the courtyard. Five poles supported the thatch roof, one at each corner, and one in the middle. The center pole had several smooth white stones, about the size of an egg, protruding from the earth. These had come along from Santal Parganas, and each represented the departed spirit of a former chieftain. Raghu firmly believed they aided in making decisions. Moreover, they bound the past to the present, thus resulting in a continuous line. But tonight the *manjhithan* sat vacant, as it had for the past two days and nights. Khanua's elders celebrated Pradhan's wedding to Manjli, beautiful daughter of a wealthy farmer who lived thirty miles southwest. For hours the Santal women sang in tones and half-tones, extolling the age-old love song of a young man finding his bride.

Pradhan found it heady, to say the least. He reveled in Manjli's beauty. True, he saw little of her, for the women were in a group apart. But among the men the bridegroom now enjoyed a camaraderie not extended prior to last month's episode with the boar. The celebration of attaining young manhood and position could easily have led to excess, except for Dulu's watchful eye. At crucial times his companion's gentle touch sufficed, that is, until the point when Pradhan sorely wanted one more drink.

"No more!" Dulu warned. "Let the others do it, but see how foolish they are acting?"

"Uh, huh!" the bridegroom responded almost belligerently. He started to say, "Dulu, leave me alone! I'm a man now!" But his companion's winsome smile broke the animosity, and Pradhan desisted.

"Your people must never see you drunk," Dulu exclaimed. You're a marked man now, marked for leadership. Watch it!"

The chief's son began to understand why his father always provided plenty of rice beer for others, but seldom partook.

The festivities concluded with the induction ceremonies. Pradhan attained the position in the council and became marked as the heir apparent to his father's position when he allowed the lobe of his right ear to be pierced. As the silver stud was inserted, the people of Khanua cheered. Pradhan, the chief's son, now knew he was destined to lead.

His chance came in a most unexpected manner.

Chapter Two
In Search of Gold

One hot afternoon, about nine months after Pradhan's wedding, Ram Das, son of the landlord who utilized Khanua's villagers as his sharecroppers, approached Raghu.

"I bear a message from my father," he said.

Raghu's eyes narrowed, and he made no move to obeisance as the young man stood above him. Instead, the chief continued to busily twist hemp, making rope.

"Did you hear me?" the proud Brahman shouted in Hindi.

"Of course," the older man replied, "but why should I respond before knowing the message? Speak on."

Ram Das shrugged, and spat on the ground to show his distaste for such mockery, but the chief neither stopped working nor lifted his eyes to the *dikku*. So the young man said haughtily, "My father wants all of your men to join the insurrectionists against the British. We're marching en masse to Saharsa tonight."

Gopal Singh's son smiled as the chief suddenly stopped his rope-making and sat still, gazing at the ground. Then Raghu spoke slowly, yet clearly, "You may tell your father that we are not insurrectionists, and that we will make no decision except through our village council."

"But when will you meet?" the young man asked anxiously.

"When the moon shines over the top of the mango grove," Raghu answered in measured tones."

"But we leave at midnight."

"We cannot meet until then, and before any decision we must have a full declaration of this venture."

"That means I talk to your council?"

"Yes, exactly!" Raghu spit a line of tobacco toward the nearby road, and it evaporated in the dust.

"In that case, I'll be back, even though I have other things to do."

"As you please," the chief responded, a wry smile flitting around his mouth.

As the moon rose over the mango trees, the circle of village elders sat in the open courtyard, not in the *manjhithan*. The stocky young Indian in his late teens waved his arms and shouted, "Gold, I tell you! For the taking! Gold, men!"

Not a person moved. As prey watching an oncoming predator, the circle of twenty Santal leaders noted Ram Das's every gesture. They remembered many empty promises.

"You don't believe me?" Ram Das challenged sharply. "Well, I'm telling you the truth."

The chief's son spoke up, "Where? Where is the gold?"

"Less than fifty miles from here. In Saharsa."

"Stop talking nonsense. There can't be mounds of money that close, available for the taking." Pradhan stood and faced his opponent.

A murmur of approval rippled through the circle. The chief's son was taking the lead, even as he did when they went on the hunt.

Ram Das tossed his head defiantly. "I'm not talking nonsense," he shouted. "Join us in our venture against the British military, and you'll return wealthy. We're going to Saharsa to loot the Treasury, and we leave at midnight. Come along!"

"Why do you want us? Take your own people," Pradhan retorted.

"Hmmm . . . why do we want you? For your bows and arrows," the young Brahman replied. "Pradhan, we know you! Don't think we're ignorant when you bring in the wild boar for your feasts. My father has been watching you! Now come with your poisoned arrows and join us . . . all of you!"

"Oh?" Pradhan looked Ram Das in the eye. "So you propose to use us to face the white man?"

"Not alone. I tell you, thousands are gathering in Saharsa tomorrow. The important thing is the money. The military is incidental. We'll loot not only the Treasury, but the Mission."

"Mission? What's that?"

"White people with their foreign religion, and wealth," he snarled. "Wealth, I tell you. They live in a palace, five minutes from the Saharsa Railway Station. They preach love and goodness. They sing songs about their God, Jesus, but you should see their luxurious house."

Ram Das paced back and forth. "What are we promising you? Gold and silver, if you'll join."

"Leave!" the chief commanded coldly. "We'll send word within the hour." Pradhan sat down beside his father and the ensuing silence shouted in its stillness. Not until the Brahman strode out of sight did the council members speak. Then a chuckle rose first from the chief, then rippled in mirth around the circle, "Like his dad, isn't he?" someone said.

"Who?"

"*Dikku!*" another said in reply.

Raghu finally spoke, "My men, I think you'd better go. I'd lead the group except for this infernal pain in my hip. It always gets worse during the monsoon." The chief turned toward his son and said, "Pradhan, you go in my stead. You're young and strong. We daren't displease our landlord. He controls our livelihood."

The council nodded affirmation, and Kailash observed, "Ram Das promises much gold and silver. Bah! How about his past record? All I can say is we've learned to distrust his words."

The chief replied, "True, Kailash, and I'm not suggesting you go for the gold or silver Ram Das promises, but rather to mollify our landlord. Do you consider that a valid reason?" A murmur of assent verified the chief's decision, and he added, "Pradhan will lead you, and believe me, the braves of Khanua match the best hunters in this whole country!"

Shortly before midnight thirty Santals, bows and arrows in hand, jogged down the path from Khanua village to Gopal Singh's cluster of houses a mile distant. The light of the moon cast shadows against the fields of grain on either side. Clouds scurried back and forth, as though empathizing with the masses of people gathering throughout the countryside below.

Excitement mounted as the crowds moved toward Saharsa.

All along the route other Santals joined with Hindu villagers. They presented a motley throng. The undisciplined and vociferous, armed with brickbats, staves and a few guns, followed the elite corps of almost four hundred Santals. Jubilant political leaders preceded the tribals. Their shouting and catchy tunes awakened the uninformed to ask, "What's happening?"

"Come and see! Money, man! Gold and silver—we're out to loot the Treasury in Saharsa and kill the missionaries. We'll be kings! Free! Finished with the white man . . . *Hindustan Zindabad!*" (Long live the land of the Hindus!)

In the midst of this seething mass of people, only the Santals moved forward silently. Most of them, like those from Khanua, farmed fertile lands for rich landlords. Past experience warned that promises could be empty, but they kept their thoughts to themselves. Gold and silver? They would see.

A runner met the mob as they neared Saharsa, "Fifty-four have come," he gasped, holding his side and trying to catch his breath. "Only two white men; all the rest, Indian brothers."

"Who?" questioned Ram Das Singh, surging forward with a group of zealous young Brahmans.

"The military! They've reached the station, on their way to the courts."

"Come on," shouted Ram Das. The crowd cheered, and broke into a run as they neared Saharsa Bazaar.

Every road and village trail reechoed with cries of "*Hindustan Zindabad!*" Thousands upon thousands converged on the little Indian town that hot August day in 1942.

"Guns first," growled the rebel leader in Pradhan's group. "Guns first, then bows and arrows."

"Stop!" an Indian magistrate ordered as he led fifty-four military police under the command of two British officers down the bazaar road.

But the mobs pressed forward. On . . . on! Past the Mission gate. They'd take care of the missionaries later. First, they must finish off these two Britishers.

"Stop!" the magistrate called the second time. "Stop, or we'll shoot!"

"We'll shoot first," a rebel leader yelled. He took aim and

shot. Others followed suit, but the Indian magistrate shouted, "Stop! If you value your lives, stop!"

"Open fire," the magistrate ordered tersely. Volleys of shots pierced the air, and villagers in the forefront began to fall. The rebel leaders quickly slithered out of the crowds to hide behind open doorways. But looking out they yelled, "On, on, men! Go after them!"

People suddenly realized they had entered a death trap as those in the oncoming ranks stumbled over those who were falling. Bullets whizzed past . . . of what use were brickbats and clubs . . . or for that matter, poisoned arrows?

Pandemonium resulted, with people fleeing everywhere . . . anywhere . . . to get out of range of those death-dealing bullets. Pradhan and Dulu, side by side, escaped but saw Manu fall. They pushed into the masses, picked him up and fought their way to the edge of the road. "Where? Where shall we take him?" Pradhan panted. "Where's the hospital?"

"The Mission compound—through that gate to the left," an old lady shouted as she peered through a partially closed window. "Come, come in quickly! I'll show you."

The Santals slipped inside, away from the mob. They carried Manu to the mission clinic where two missionary men and a foreign nurse already ministered to the wounded. The lady's face blanched as the crowd continued to grow, but this was no time for weakness. She cleansed Manu's wound with swift, sure strokes, applied medication and bound it with a clean, white bandage. Tumultuous thoughts surged through Pradhan's mind as he watched the compassion on the white lady's face. Did these foreigners know the crowds expected to kill them? If so, why were they here ministering instead of hiding? Was it greed for financial gain?

Pradhan fingered his money bag at his waist and asked, "How much do we owe?"

"Nothing," the lady said with a smile. "We do this because we love Jesus."

"Please take something for the medicine," he urged, handing her a *rupee*. "You'll be treating many today." His eyes gleamed as he thanked her.

Dulu said softly, "You go ahead, Pradhan, and tell the chief.

Manu shouldn't force himself right now. I'll stay with him and come later." Pradhan nodded, then left.

"How much gold did you get, son?" the chief asked as he twisted strands of hemp together to make rope. He looked up from his mat on the verandah in the early evening.

Pradhan grunted, and placed his bow and arrows on the verandah. "Gold? Empty promises, sir."

"No pockets filled with gold?"

"No, Dad. We faced guns . . . never saw the Treasury!"

"Guns?" The chief looked up with interest. "The military?"

"Yes, Dad. Over fifty Indians, fully armed. Only two white men. An Indian gave the order to fire, and many died. Our arrows fell short in the face of guns." The young man paused, unsure how to proceed. "Manu fell . . ."

"Manu? Our Manu?"

"Yes, sir. Dulu and I carried him to a hospital clinic on the Mission compound. A white lady bound his wound and treated us kindly. Several white men helped with other patients."

"How many casualties, son?"

"About thirty waiting when we were there, I'd guess."

"The white people cared for you?"

"Yes, Dad."

The chief looked up slyly. White men live for money, he knew, so he asked, "How much did it cost?"

"Nothing! I gave her a *rupee*, to help pay for the medicine, and she thanked me."

"They must be very rich to provide medical care without charging. What's their game?" Raghu rose from his sitting posture, put the hemp rope in a basket on the verandah and began rolling a cigarette.

Pradhan answered quietly, "She said they're doing it for the love of Jesus, sir."

"Jesus? Their God?"

"Yes, Dad."

"Hmmm . . ." Khanua's chief grunted thoughtfully as he lit his cigarette and inhaled deeply.

Chapter Three

The Drum Beats

"Dhuka-da-duk, dhuka-da-duk, dhuka-da-duk," the drum beats rolled on a glorious autumn night in Khanua village. In the commons two long lines of figures, one for men, the other women, wove back and forth to the beating of the drums and the fine singing of female voices. Arms around one another's waists, the lines flowed and moved like a serpent.

Tonight's festivities celebrated not only the rice harvest, but the birth of Pradhan and Manjli's first son. Pradhan provided the venison and his father an abundance of rice beer.

Ram Das Singh watched from the shadows, then returned home to report to his father. "They're drunk, Dad," he said succinctly. "You won't get a *pice* of work out of any of them for three days!"

"But they've been at this for three days already," the older man growled. "What's going on?"

"A double celebration, apparently," his son replied.

"What?"

"The harvest, of course. We expected that, but now it seems Pradhan has a son, so Raghu's gone all out—he's a grandpa now."

"Well, I don't blame him. And I like Pradhan."

"I don't! He had the nerve to face me on that Saharsa deal." Ram Das shrugged, then added, "I'd like to cut him down to size."

"But he's one of my best workers."

"That doesn't mean a thing, Dad. You're the landlord, aren't you? So he's going to stay on the good side of you. See?"

In the village, festivities continued far into the night. Plenty

13

of venison and rice beer effectively minimized the world's problems, not to mention their own.

One story called forth spontaneous laughter—the time they pursued the wrong game. "Never again!" Kailash exclaimed. "We know better now. Gold and silver? Ha! Ha!" And Manu replied, "What wealth did I get? Just this." He touched his side where he bore the scar.

Their listeners, half drunk, roared with mirth and again recited the empty promises Ram Das had made. They concluded, "Never again! We're Santals, not *dikkus*." Pradhan listened and watched a bit sadly. Were they acting as true men when they allowed the rice beer to control? He glanced at Dulu, as usual sitting by his side, and an understanding smile passed between them.

"Dhuka-da-duk, dhuka-da-duk," the drum beats rolled one particular evening as twilight lengthened into night. Men and women congregated quickly on the large commons near the chief's home. The rhythm announced a festive occasion, so the villagers came lightheartedly.

Pradhan and Dulu joined several other young men who surrounded a guest. He sat crosslegged on a wooden bed. His white hair fell gently around his shoulders; his long, flowing beard rested on his chest. Beside him lay a cane and a small bundle that apparently held his belongings.

"What is your name?" the chief's son inquired respectfully.

The old man's eyes twinkled as he answered, "*Haram* (old man), my child."

"Haram?" The young men chuckled, and Pradhan tried again. "Of course you're an old man, father, but what is your name?"

"I told you. Haram."

"Well, then, how old are you?"

Haram laughed, then answered, "How can I tell? Maybe I've been here forever. . . ."

Pradhan drew back, startled, then drew closer to hear his guest say, "Yet I do remember my youth. Yes . . . it was back in our homeland, Santal Parganas. When I was your age, my boys, I brought in the wild boar for our feasts. And I sat at the feet of another *haram* who spun tales about our people. When he died, I became his mouthpiece."

"The chief's coming," Dulu whispered to Pradhan who drew back immediately to allow his father to approach.

The chief bowed low before Haram and said, "I'm happy to meet you, father."

The old man returned the blessing by extending his right hand, left hand touching his right elbow, in the ceremonial Santal fashion. With a smile he said, "It's my pleasure, son."

Taking a seat at one edge of the bed, the chief continued, "Your fame in storytelling has preceded you, so I've called my people together. I trust you aren't too weary?"

"I'll be ready as soon as you are," he said with a twinkle.

By this time Pradhan's mother made her way through the gathering crowd to the guest. He swung around and placed his dusty feet in the gleaming brass plate she set before him on the ground. With water from another brass container she washed the guest's feet, then withdrew, only to return with a cup of steaming hot tea. He took it gratefully, and the chief conversed with him as he drank.

"I believe you travel extensively?" Raghu asked.

"Yes . . . wherever my people migrate."

"Where have you come from now?"

"For the last two moons I've lived among Santals working in the tea gardens to the east, and also found large pockets of migrants across our northern borders."

"You mean in Nepal, respected father?"

"Yes, my son. Many live in the hill country to the north of our land. They look upon Santal Parganas as their homeland but many have little or no knowledge of our traditions or ways. I wandered their hamlets and trails for a full moon."

Pradhan edged closer and asked, "But why do you take so much trouble? Wouldn't you like to stay home with your family and friends?"

"I must perform my mission, lad," Haram said as he looked indulgently at the questioner. He liked this tall youth, marked for leadership with the silver stud in his right ear. Haram noted

Pradhan's genteel ways, touched however with the courage and arrogance of youth, and he smiled. "My son, I was once like you," he said, "until I sat at the feet of another *haram*. What he told me changed my life. Perhaps what I tell you will change yours. Let us now begin."

The bard of undetermined age settled himself more securely on the wooden bed, crossing his legs in a lotus-like position. He raised his hand for silence, and the waiting crowd that had squatted on the ground listened intently to his opening remarks.

"I must tell stories of our ancient past. It is easy, so very easy to forget our heritage."

"Well said, father," the chief commented. "These young fellows learn Hindi and too soon become part of the *dikkus*. Tell them, Haram."

The old man nodded, then closed his eyes and snapped his fingers to set the rhythm. His quavery voice rose in a plaintive ode to the Great Spirit—tones and half-tones rising and falling within a six-tone scale. After his song he leaned forward and said, "Ah, my children, I must introduce you to Thakur Jiu. You haven't heard of him? No? This is why I have come—to proclaim his name."

The bard spoke with arms extended, "Far, far west of this great nation lies our first homeland. The first man and woman, Haram and Ayo, lived in Hihiri Pipri. And, you ask, who created them? Thakur Jiu, the Great Spirit!

"Thakur Jiu is before all others. He lives far above the heavens and the earth." He lifted his arms, and looking upward continued, "I bring you his name—Thakur Jiu. He is greater than any spirit. He sees all, upholds, and nourishes all."

A rustle of interest rippled through the crowd. Haram nodded and smiled, then continued, "Our forefathers knew him and worshiped him." Now the old man dropped his arms, gazed at his audience and whispered forlornly, "But you don't even know his name? Oh, my children, we have lost him! We have replaced the knowledge of the True One with the worship of the *bongas* (evil spirits) and *Marang Buru* (Great Mountain).

Haram paused, then broke into song, the story of a lost love. He leaned forward after singing and asked, "How did it happen? Ah, my children . . . listen . . . Thakur Jiu's enemy, Lita, came to tempt Haram and Ayo, our forefathers. 'Make me some rice beer,' he said. 'Pour it on the ground as an offering to Satan.'

" 'Satan?' Haram and Ayo asked. 'Who's he?'

" 'Greater than Thakur Jiu,' this strange, beautiful creature replied. 'He is wiser than all, and sees all.'

"Haram and Ayo made the rice beer, then offered it by pouring some on the ground to Satan. They drank the rest with frenzy, then sank into a drunken sleep. When they awoke, they realized they were naked and for the first time, they were ashamed."

"Ah, ha!" breathed Haram's audience in empathy of spirit. What would a wedding be without plenty of rice beer? Or any festival for that matter? Hadn't they recently drunk to the full when they celebrated the harvest and the birth of Pradhan's first son?

The old man continued the story. "Haram and Ayo's seven sons and daughters migrated eastward, always toward the rising sun. They bore sons and daughters, and each son used his bow and arrow well. But these mighty men became corrupted with rice beer. Each day they poured a little on the ground to Satan, then drank the rest. Yet they still knew Thakur Jiu's name.

"But great sorrow now filled Thakur Jiu's heart. He called men to repent, to return to his love. But only two people still loved him, so he hid them in a cave in Mount Harata and destroyed the rest in a mighty flood."

"Ohh . . ." An audible sigh swept through the crowd. Pradhan felt an inward tug, a twinge of pain.

Haram closed his eyes again, then sang to the snapping of his fingers. "Thakur Jiu is great. He is merciful and kind, saving his people from total destruction."

"Are you weary?" the old man asked.

"Weary?" the people said, astonished. "We could listen all night. More, please!"

He turned toward Raghu, and the chief nodded, so Haram smiled, stroked his long white beard and said, "More? Yes, children, there is more, much more. Listen . . .

"Our forefathers multiplied again after the flood. They moved to a great plain where Thakur Jiu separated peoples, giving each a distinct language. He assigned them a homeland

and said Santals would find theirs toward the rising sun." The bard stopped, then asked, "Have you ever felt compelled to move east? Yes? Well, that's the reason." He paused, then continued, "Our long pilgrimage began. Our people traveled over scorching sands. They crossed great rivers, only to arrive at the highest mountains on earth."

"Ohh . . ." again that audible sigh.

"Day after day they sought an opening. Hope finally gave way to despair. The mountains were too tall, too strong, yet our Santal homeland lay on the other side."

"Ah, ha!" A ripple of empathy passed through the crowd, and they leaned forward to hear Haram's wistful lyric of longing for home. Who among them hadn't felt it? Pradhan and Dulu, seated on a mat near the bed were particularly moved.

The bard gave his full attention to the crowd and with a piercing gaze proclaimed, "My children, listen to me! That's when it happened! We sold our heritage. Not to Lita . . . no, Satan is too clever for that. He takes many disguises. Now he comes as the beautiful 'Spirit of the Mountains.' We call him *Marang Buru*."

A solemn hush fell on the audience. Raghu shifted uneasily, but didn't disturb Haram who whispered pensively, "The spirit spoke persuasively. He said, 'Follow me, my friends. I know the route and I'll guide you. See? I'm greater than your Thakur Jiu. I'm your deliverer. Leave Thakur Jiu and worship me. I'll take you across the mountains.' "

A deep sigh rippled through the audience, and again the chief's son felt a foreboding of evil, something sinister that mounted as the ancient bard continued. The old man hunched forward, his eyes gleaming. "And what did our forefathers do? Did they pact with Satan?"

Every head nodded affirmation.

"Yes, we did it. We left Thakur Jiu for his arch-enemy. It is true *Marang Buru* is great. He led us through the great mountains to our homeland south of the Ganges, but we forfeited the worship and knowledge of the True One. We lost our heritage! Oh, my children . . . my children," the bard wailed, "is it to be forever?"

Haram closed his eyes and sang a lament, then concluded in a hushed tone, "I do not believe it is for ever. The True One can never forget us. Surely, if we seek him, he will come and deliver us from slavery to the evil one."

The man sank back, exhausted. Pradhan, Dulu, and several others rushed forward to help him.

"Come, come, my friend," Raghu said quickly, "how unthinking we have been not to feed you first. Thank you for coming. Now you must eat."

The villagers rose and stretched, then dispersed. But Pradhan aided Haram to a chair that Dulu brought from inside the house. "Tell me, my father," Pradhan said as he leaned over the weary traveler, "is it only a story?"

"My son, I believe it to be true, but who can tell? These are the legends we heard from our elders. We can but pass them on to our children and grandchildren."

"You don't worship *Marang Buru?*"

The old man's eyes glistened with unshed tears, "No," he whispered to the two young men before him. "Ever since I left chasing the wild boar to roam these trails, I have given my heart to Thakur Jiu. I long to know him again. I believe he will find us, his people. We are lost, but let us search. He will free us from Satan's grasp."

The chief walked briskly onto the verandah and said, "Come, come, Dulu and Pradhan. You weary our guest unduly. Bring him inside for his food."

Some weeks later the drum beats rolled again, this time with ominous sound. "Dhuka-da-da-da-duk, dhuka-da-da-da-duk." The villagers heard it fearfully, and in answer to the summons all hastened to the chief's courtyard, even though it was mid-morning. The men squatted together on the ground, the women stood at a discreet distance, faces partially covered with the cotton shawls they used for blouses.

In the *manjhithan*, the chief and members of council took their places in a circle around the central pole. Several men danced around the pole to the accelerated beat of the drums, "Dhuka-da-da-da-duk, dhuka-da-da-da-duk."

"What is it?" Dulu questioned Pradhan as he sat to the immediate left of the chief's son.

"I don't know," he answered grimly. His father's face seemed set, inscrutable.

Raghu nodded to the drummers, and in the eerie silence that followed, he spoke loudly, "Smallpox has broken out in Kailu's house. The *bongas* are displeased because we listened to Haram's stories, and they have planted a witch among us. She is doing much harm."

Women disappeared behind walls, faces suddenly drawn in fear. The chief continued, "The witch has connived evil to Kailu's family. She probably plans to harm all of us. Who will volunteer to visit the witch doctor? We must find the witch!"

Kailu, seated outside the *manjhithan*, rose. He was a tall man, strong and handsome, and known for his industrious ways. But fear now flickered in his eyes, and he winced at the chief's words. He knew Raghu expected him to volunteer. Likely doing so would lead to further implications, but Kailu felt he had no other recourse. So he rose and signed assent.

The crowd dispersed without the usual banter and laughter. Kailu and two friends soon went to the witch doctor, bearing chickens for sacrifice to the *bongas*, and plenty of money for the priest.

Pradhan returned slowly to the field where he had left his plow and oxen. His thoughts whirled. A witch! It could be any of the women. Perhaps his mother? Or his beautiful wife Manjli, mother of his son Jatha?

The young man's shoulders sagged as though carrying a heavy load to market. Yet that would be nothing, he concluded, nothing at all in comparison to his burden of fear and distrust.

Every Santal knew that witches connived with the evil spirits at night, then returned to serve as dutiful wives during the day. That's why a man must always distrust a woman! He shuddered and felt the forces of evil were too strong for him to face. Yet where could he find release?

The chief's son glanced across the field to the *sal* tree, considered sacred as the abode of the *bongas*. A small pile of crushed brick lay at its base, with the hope that the inquisitive spirits would stop to count before proceeding into the village for their night's frolic. Perhaps that would help to allay the mischief. Pradhan walked over and threw several more pieces on the pile, then returned to his plow.

Kailu and his friends returned the next morning to find his wife tenderly caring for their sick child. How could he beat her? Yet the witch doctor had designated her as the witch!

His two companions noted Kailu's reluctance. Obviously he needed help, so they fed him plenty of rice beer. Then, urging him on, they accompanied him as he raged into the house and beat the woman who had mothered his three children. She fled the village, screaming.

Kailu sank upon a mat in a drunken stupor and slept. But when he awoke, his head pounded and his guilt-ridden conscience cried out, "Thakur Jiu, where are you?"

He would have been amazed to know that Thakur Jiu was already planning to invade Khanua.

Chapter Four

Benjamin,
Converted Witch Doctor

Several hundred miles south of Khanua, beyond the great river Ganges, Benjamin Marandi awoke to another day. He rubbed his eyes, sat on the rope bed in the open courtyard where he had slept to get the benefit of any passing breeze, and picked up his violin from its place on the bamboo mat. A haunting melody of praise soon mingled with the resonant cooing of the doves in the nearby *matkon* trees.

Here in Santal Parganas this white-haired gentleman exerted considerable influence. His fields surrounded his spacious adobe house and courtyard, but he was known for traits other than farming. Benjamin had been a *jan guru*, a leader of witch doctors in Santal Parganas. In those days he served the *bongas* wholeheartedly, beating the rhythms all night and preparing chickens for sacrifice with bare hands.

But his conversion to Jesus Christ electrified his people. Some threatened his life, others followed his example. Now he traversed the area with his violin and homespun illustrations. Gently, but persistently, he probed the consciences of the people as he told them of Thakur Jiu, the Great Spirit.

At the beginning of this new day, Benjamin again thanked God for release from the bondage of Satan, and for Jesus Christ, his Liberator. An hour of reading the Scriptures, mingled with prayer and praise, passed quickly. Suddenly a strident voice from the back of the house interrupted his devotions. "Here, Bellamdina, take this tea to your father. I can't imagine why he's not come for breakfast. It's late, and I have a lot of work to do."

The man smiled. Would his wife never understand? But Bellamdina—well, she was different. His nineteen-year-old and he shared an empathy of spirit that he found lacking in his wife and son. Perhaps it stemmed from character likenesses, but he strongly suspected that the bond came from his daughter's firm personal faith in Jesus as her Lord. He prayed for Sarah and Solomon daily, that they would get beyond a nominal adherence to Christianity and walk into a vital relationship with Jesus.

As he was musing on this, Bellamdina approached with a smile. She moved with light steps, bearing a tray. Her pink *sari* was tastefully draped, and her black hair combed neatly into a braid down her back.

"Good morning, Papa," she said blithely, placing the tray beside him. "Are you feeling well?"

"Good morning, my girl. Yes, I'm fine," he responded as he laid his Bible down. He looked at her and asked, "Why, daughter? Is something wrong?"

The girl hesitated, then sat on the mat at his feet. She said, "Mama thinks you're getting lazier every day. It's hard to keep still when I know it isn't laziness. You're talking to God!"

"She means well, Bellamdina," the elderly man responded gently. "She works hard, and your mother and brother have made this farm prosper. I certainly can't take much credit."

"Oh, but Papa," she cried, "you have far greater work to do. Anyone can farm, but not everyone can tell how the Lord saved them from *Marang Buru*. I think that's terribly important."

He hesitated before answering, and the girl sensed he had something to share, so she waited. When he spoke he said, "My girl, what if the Lord sends me away from home?"

"What do you mean? You aren't home much now, Papa. You're out with your violin and Bible."

He felt a tug around his heart, something akin to physical pain, but he continued, "Bellamdina, as much as I enjoy my home and family, my Lord is calling me to something else."

"Why, Papa?" she cried in alarm. "What have we done?"

"Nothing, daughter. It's not your fault. God is calling me. Remember Samuel? How God spoke to him at night?"

"Yes. . . ." She waited while he fingered his violin strings. He seemed far away. "Has something special happened?" she asked.

"The Lord called me in a dream last night," he replied. "I can see every detail now. He told me that thousands of our people are still without any chance to hear the gospel. They long to know him, but there's nobody to tell them. Here in Santal Parganas we have missionaries and many churches. But North Bihar is new territory. I must go north of the river, Bellamdina. God has called."

His wife's voice suddenly demanded attention, "Bellamdina, you lazy girl! What are you doing? Come here immediately!"

Benjamin looked up and smiled as she stood to her feet. "You must understand her, my dear," he urged softly. "She means well."

"I know, and I try to help all I can."

"Well, hold your tongue, and don't mention the dream."

"I won't, Papa." The girl turned to go, then added, "If you leave Santal Parganas, I want to go along to take care of you."

Five miles to the west, Hanikhol village prepared for the one major excitement of the day, the arrival of the express bus from Bhagalpur bound for Dumka, the District Headquarters. It brought the daily newspaper with news of the outside world. Strangers would sometimes drop interesting information while sipping hot tea at one of the busy tea stalls.

Three local busses, rusty and creaking, stood awaiting transfer of passengers. Bystanders made idle talk around the various booths. Each pulled his thin sheet around his shoulders to thwart the morning chill.

The express pulled in with a flourish, and passengers descended into the ranks of shrouded villagers. The tea stalls suddenly teemed with customers. Vendors sold food and trinkets to those travelers who preferred holding seats by occupancy. Seats were always in high demand. In fact, only the fortunate enjoyed them. Most passengers stood throughout the six-hour ride.

A stranger approached the corner tea stall. His sharp features and clipped Hindi marked him as from a far country. Chatter ceased when he asked, "Friends, could any of you help me find Benjamin Marandi, a former witch doctor?"

The Santals glanced at each other but none spoke. Who among them didn't know the witch doctor? They had sought him out before with their money. Now he sought them out with his persuasive arguments against the religion of the *bongas*. He shook their foundations!

The stranger waited, but not meeting with response, turned to the shopkeeper and requested, "Please, sir, I'd like a cup of tea and some *purees* (bread) with potato curry."

He sensed a general rustle of interest. One man asked, "You've come from Bhagalpur?"

"No, from far beyond that—from north of the Ganges."

"Oh," they breathed, as though it was some foreign land. "What is it like?"

"Very different from your homeland," the stranger said with a smile. "It's flat—not a hill in sight."

"Could it be?" the man answered, and everyone laughed.

The stranger continued, "Yes, it's flat, but rich for farming. We have good crops and heavy rainfall, also floods. That brings both blessing and hardship."

The Santals nodded, then asked, "Since you come from such a distant country, how do you know Benjamin Marandi?"

"We worked together in Bhagalpur," he said. "When our assignment finished, I returned north, and he came here. I haven't seen him since."

An elderly man spoke up. "I know him well. In fact, he came to my village last week and we lunched together after his public meeting. Take the road to where it forks, but leave both main trails. Follow the footpath to the left, through the fields to the group of palms on the hill. Walk about three miles beyond that to Pipri village. If you inquire there, someone will direct you to his house."

"Oh, thank you, my brother," the stranger said gratefully. "God bless you."

He picked up his umbrella and shoulder bag, nodded to the group and sauntered over to a nearby hand-pump. After washing face and hands, he shook the dust from his shirt that had accrued through hours of night travel over bumpy roads. He would have preferred to sleep, but aware that the sun's hot rays would deter his progress, the stranger began his trek.

As he neared Pipri village, he squinted up at the sun and

surmised, "Must be about ten o'clock. I hope Benjamin is still home."

The stranger stopped to mop his brow and sat a few minutes in the shade of some bamboo clumps. They stood straight and tall, their graceful, feathery leaves hanging like a fringe and quivering with the slightest breeze. The man watched them appreciatively, noting their beauty.

It's like God's working, he mused. He's there . . . he's moving . . . I hear the sound, but I don't see his face. Lord, he prayed, guide me to Benjamin. You've brought me thus far.

Refreshed from that moment of contemplation, the man arose and continued his journey. Soon he spotted a Santal in a nearby field. "I'm looking for Benjamin Marandi," he said as he approached. "Does he live in this village?"

"Yes, sir," the young man replied.

"Why, I believe you resemble him!"

The young man smiled. "He's my father, sir. I'm Solomon Marandi. And you?" he asked.

"Isaac Paul, a preacher from North Bihar. I knew your father when he worked in the leprosarium in Bhagalpur."

"Glad to meet you, sir," the young man answered in clear Hindi, so unlike the market variety Isaac had heard earlier this morning.

"God is good! I prayed the Lord to guide me, and he has. Praise the Lord! Where's your home?"

"Just follow me."

Women and children turned to watch the stranger as the two men entered the village. "*Dikku!*" they said. Dogs barked, then backed away. Isaac strode confidently toward Benjamin's house.

Benjamin arose from sitting on the rope bed that had now been pulled under the shade of a large mango tree. He extended his right arm in greeting as the men approached and called, "Welcome, welcome, my brother!"

"Pastor Benjamin, is it really you?"

"Yes, Isaac. So this is the reason the Lord wouldn't allow me to go to the villages today. Usually I'm out, you know."

"Well, I'm glad you're here. Three years hasn't aged you a bit."

"Never felt better, thank God. Come, come, my brother. Sit

and rest yourself. You must be very weary from your journey." He turned to Solomon and said, "Tell your mother we have a guest, son." Then he called as an afterthought, "Bring a chair, please."

Five minutes later Sarah hurried toward the visitor, in her hands a highly polished brass plate and vessel containing water. She placed Isaac's dusty feet onto the plate, then washed them with the cooling liquid.

This welcome ritual accomplished, Benjamin's wife served tea to the visitor and her husband.

Solomon stood to one side. As Isaac glanced at father and son he noted an even stronger resemblance than his first impression . . . same high cheek bones, same wide forehead and flared nostrils, and same medium brown color. But the father's relaxed smile and humble manner indicated he had lived long enough to learn that true leadership serves another. His son portrayed the confidence of youth, pride written over his handsome features.

Isaac drew an envelope from his inner pocket. "I've brought you a letter, Benjamin," he said. "This will explain my visit."

The white-haired gentleman tore it open and read, "We need someone to help in our evangelistic work, and Isaac Paul suggested your name. We're camped in an area where many Santals come to market, and their obvious interest in the gospel demands that we try to meet their needs. Yet they fail to catch our Hindi. Will you join us for several weeks, dear brother?" It bore the signature of an American missionary.

Benjamin looked up and asked, "When would you like me to come?"

"As soon as possible," Isaac said quietly. "We've been in camp for the past week, and I'd like to return as quickly as you will permit me to leave. There's great interest! It's phenomenal, a real challenge."

Benjamin broke into a chuckle and said, "Don't think I'll permit you to go alone, brother Isaac. As soon as my wife brings that chicken curry and we eat our lunch, we can be on our way." He added thoughtfully, "I believe we can still catch the late afternoon bus to Bhagalpur."

Isaac blinked in surprise, then laughed and said, "Pastor

Benjamin! You don't even know where you're going!" But the converted witch doctor chuckled again and observed, "No need. The Lord has given me my orders."

Solomon listened in amazement. Was his father out of his mind? How could he walk away from home and responsibilities? Benjamin must have sensed his son's uneasiness. "Come here," he said.

The young man walked over to his father, and Benjamin reached out and touched him. "I've been watching you, my boy, and you're doing very well on the farm. With your mother's guidance, you can handle things without me for several weeks. I'm proud of you, Solomon."

The young man straightened, and his eyes shone. His father continued, "I know this sounds unusual, but there's a compulsion about this call that demands my obedience. The Lord showed me last night that I must leave to go north of the river and preach to my people."

Benjamin turned to Isaac, his black eyes twinkling. "Oh, yes, there is one question. Where is the camp? I must be sure this is God's choice. It would be bad to go to the wrong place."

Isaac and Solomon laughed heartily, and Benjamin sensed his son's antipathy had diminished. Isaac answered, "The camp? It's north of the Ganges, Benjamin. About twenty, or maybe thirty years ago, thousands of your people migrated to clear jungle land and begin farming. They live among Hindus and Muslims, but don't understand our language very well. So we need your help. You'll make an invaluable member of our team."

"The right place," the converted witch doctor said with an affirming nod of his head. "Let me collect my blanket, a change of clothing and some money. Yes, I'll join you. But first, you must sleep a little. Then we'll eat lunch and be on our way."

While Isaac slept and Solomon returned to the field for an hour's work, Benjamin broke the news to his wife and daughter. He was rather surprised at Sarah's reaction. Small in stature, and of a propensity to hard work, she said caustically, "Well, you might as well go. We're not getting any work out of you these days in any case."

"Mama!"

She swung around to find Bellamdina behind her. "What do you want, girl?"

"I heard what Papa said, and I'll help while he's gone. You and Solomon can work in the fields, and I'll do everything here at home. I think God's work is very important, isn't it?"

The woman felt caught, so she said no more, but busied herself with her cooking.

Several hours later the two men strode down the dusty trail toward Hanikhol village where they would catch the late afternoon bus for Bhagalpur. Benjamin's daughter watched them go, and with great yearning whispered, "Lord, Papa needs someone to care for him. If you're taking him north of the river to live, couldn't I accompany him? Please, God."

The weeks passed by slowly for Dina (Solomon's nickname for his sister.) Several weeks later she recognized a white-haired gentleman carrying a violin. She bounded down the village path and called, "Papa, Papa, you've come!"

"Yes, daughter. Is everything all right at home?"

When they met she answered, "Yes, we've gotten along fine. Solomon and Mama worked in the fields each day, and I stayed in the house. So I've prayed a lot, and thought a great deal. And you know what, Papa? I'm coming with you! I'm coming, too! The Lord told me I may go."

"Yes?" he queried with a smile at her eagerness. "How do you know I'm returning?"

She laughed, a joyous, tinkling sound, then said, "The Lord told me."

"That's confirmation," he replied with a chuckle. "Yes, I'm going, Bellamdina, and I want to take both your mother and you to live there."

"Mama? Will she go?"

"We'll see. At least we must give her the chance."

"And Solomon?"

"We'll hurry his wedding date. He can live here with his bride and care for the farm. Even if your mother wants to come back occasionally, she can do so. She gets along fine with Solomon."

"But maybe she'll hear God call, too, and want to stay, Papa," his daughter responded wistfully.

With misty eyes he answered, "Let's pray about it."

Two months later, after the wedding, Benjamin left the bride and groom on the farm. With his wife and daughter, he moved north of the Ganges River to begin a ministry that extended through many years.

It began in Khanua.

Chapter Five

The New Neighbors

One midmorning, Raghu sat at the edge of the threshing floor outside the village, supervising his three sons, aged eleven to fifteen. While Salku drove the oxen round and round, his brothers kept stirring the ripened grain with sticks. Puchu suddenly shouted, "Look! A white man is coming!"

Two cyclists approached, one a foreigner of distinguished appearance, his face leathery with a permanent tan from living long years in India. He wore a khaki shirt and shorts, open sandals, and pith helmet covering his greying hair. His companion, an Indian of round face and pleasant countenance, wore the traditional white cotton shirt and *dhoti*. As the travelers neared, the Indian asked in halting Santali, "Is this Khanua village?"

The boys giggled in surprise, and this called forth a further effort on the man's part. "So you're doing a fine job for your father?"

They nodded, and the man continued, "I'm Samuel Roy from Madhipura, and my friend here is the Dick Sahib from Saharsa."

"Glad to meet you, boys," the foreigner said in excellent Hindi. He pushed his khaki helmet back to mop his perspiring brow, then removed his glasses and wiped them with his white handkerchief, much to the amusement of the chief's sons. "Is this Khanua?" he asked.

Civility demanded an answer, so Raghu said, "Yes, sir. Who are you looking for?"

"Guru Marandi, please."

"He's my elder brother. One of the boys will take you. Puchu, you go." He pointed to the youngest who immediately let out a whoop and joined the cyclists with joy.

31

That noon, after hearing a full report from his son, Raghu decided to talk to Guru about the incident. Opportunity came that evening when the brothers met for their usual cup of tea. Raghu began by asking casually, "Who were your visitors, and what did they want?"

Guru, shorter than Raghu and darker in color, replied, "The white man's a missionary from Saharsa; the other man lives in Madhipura."

"Oh? They're Christians?"

"Well, the foreigner is. Aren't all white people Christians?"

Raghu shrugged, faced his brother directly and asked, "What are you doing with Christians?"

The little man slapped his knee and laughed. "Look at you, Raghu, getting fussed up because the Dick Sahib comes here to visit. What am I doing with Christians? Nothing—nothing at all. I happened to meet him last month in Saharsa Bazaar when I went on business, and I learned he had treated some of our young men in the mission clinic when the *dikkus* faced the military."

"So what did you do?"

The chief rose from his mat on the verandah and stretched, then turned to fix his brother with a penetrating gaze.

Guru, lolling against the tree trunk, answered, "I did what any decent Santal would do—thanked him for caring for our people, and invited him to stop in and see us if he's ever over this way."

"Well, what do they want? Are they paying us to change our religion?"

Guru chuckled and said, "Raghu! Whatever makes you ask? That's ridiculous!"

The chief shrugged, then sat down again and replied, "The Christians in Tinkonwa village are paying the Santals. Durga told me he's changed over so that he can get a good education."

"Raghu," his brother pleaded, "please understand. Nobody's paying me any money to change my religion. My guests and I had a nice talk together, and I served them tea. Can't we be friendly even though we're different?"

The chief grunted. He extracted some tobacco from his pouch, carefully hand-rolled a cigarette while Guru watched him. Then Raghu lit the cigarette and drew a long puff before answering. As he exhaled and watched the vapor rise, he sighed and said, "The *bongas* planted a witch when we listened to Haram. What will they do now?"

"Nothing, Raghu," Guru answered. "It was a casual visit."

"But I suspect it to be more," the chief replied.

The cyclists returned several times, once accompanied by another white Sahib, but on no occasion did they exert pressure on either the chief or his family. Raghu's apprehension gradually lessened. He began to welcome the white man.

But one day their new friends informed the chief and Guru that they had bought land near Khanua. They would soon open a mission.

Chief and people stood aghast! A mission? Guru decided he had gone beyond discretion in championing their cause. Secretly, he desired to believe in the Christians' God, but now he retreated behind a hastily raised screen of indifference, dreading his brother's displeasure.

Pradhan also struggled. He definitely resented any pressure that would further displease the *bongas*. Yet he kept wondering whether the white man, coming from the west, might possibly know the true God, Thakur Jiu. Could it be that westerners retained the secret the Santals had lost?

The mission grew before their eyes—several houses for living quarters, built with mud walls and thatch roofs, a deep well, and a schoolhouse much like the *manjhithan*, but larger. It had a raised floor, open sides, and poles to support the rafters.

One unforgettable day for Khanua, Benjamin Marandi arrived with his wife and daughter. "They've come! They've come! They're not *dikkus*—they're Santals, like us!"

Young men warmly welcomed the new family and helped unload the oxcarts. "Where did you live before?" Kailu asked, as the group chatted with Benjamin after carrying in furniture and setting it in place.

"In Santal Parganas," he answered, and proceeded to enthrall them with stories of the homeland. Before long he brought out his violin and sang and played for them, to their obvious enjoyment.

As for Dina, she made friends with the women quickly, assuring them that their new well would be open to everybody.

They said gratefully, "We've had to walk a long ways when ours went dry. This is much closer."

But for the next week one subject dominated conversations around Khanua's cow dung fires. Why would anybody move here from Santal Parganas since the jungles had been cleared? Yet, Benjamin's stories passed from mouth to mouth, with alacrity and appreciation.

The second night after their arrival, Dina walked over to her father in the schoolhouse and asked, "Papa, when may I open the school? The children are asking."

He beamed, and as was his habit, blinked several times. Then he chuckled, and replied, "It is good, Bellamdina. Start as soon as you like." He touched his violin and continued, "And I'll get my literacy class organized. There are nice young men here. I'm surprised that none of them know how to read and write. No school in this village at all! We must correct that quickly, and my friend will help. We'll use the song book for our text, and my violin's sweet voice will banish fear. Yes, it is good."

Good for father and daughter, but a far different story for the remaining member of the team.

"Aren't you eating?" Benjamin asked Sarah on the third day.

"No!" she exclaimed. "There's nothing in this godforsaken place! Nothing decent! Why did I ever come?"

"My dear," her husband replied, "we have plenty of rice and potatoes, and we can grow vegetables. More than that, I'll bring you meat from market regularly. Surely you can manage."

"Maybe you can," she retorted. "If you were the least bit sensible, you'd stay in Santal Parganas for my sake. You can work for God there. The Almighty knows you're always in the villages anyway . . . but at least I had my work and my friends. I don't have anything here!"

Benjamin blinked in alarm and tried to comfort her. "Try it for my sake, Sarah," he pleaded. "You can help me, you know. The ladies need you to tell them about Jesus."

"Bellamdina's good at that," she said sniffling. She wiped her eyes with the end of her *sari* and blurted out, "I want to go home!"

"Try to be happy here," Benjamin urged. "Why should we divide the family?"

The little woman stomped her foot. "Nonsense!" she

snapped. "You can live here if you want. I can't stop you, but as for me, I'm leaving."

"Solomon will have to come for you, Sarah. Bellamdina and I have our work to do. We can't go with you."

"Then write Solomon," she insisted.

The letter went into the mail that day, but she had to wait several weeks until Solomon arrived.

"What took so long, son?" his mother asked.

"I had to bring my mother-in-law, Mom," he said gently. "My wife can't stay alone any more than you can travel on your own."

"Well, it seemed forever! Believe me, I'll be glad to get back in God's own country!"

Since any news about the newcomers held priority in Khanua's courtyards, the Santal women questioned Dina when they went to the mission well to draw water. "Your mother's leaving?" they asked.

"Yes," Dina answered. "We have our own farm in Santal Parganas, so mother will help my brother and his wife."

"Oh," they replied, "and you? Aren't you going?"

The girl's eyes sparkled as she said, "No, I'm not going. My father and I will stay."

"But don't you want to get married? All girls your age get married."

"My father needs me, and this is more important."

"But what will you do here?"

Dina waved her hand toward the school and answered, "I'm already busy teaching your children to read and write. Isn't that good?"

The women nodded and returned to the village to talk over what they had heard. Dina, in turn, took her filled clay pots to the house where her brother Solomon sat on the verandah. He watched her ascend the steps, then place her water pots on the floor. "Dina," he said, "this is a godforsaken spot. No trees, just open fields. . . ."

She laughed, a tinkling sound, and said, "You're partially right, Sol, but you forget these people have recently cleared the jungle. You see, the trees are growing, especially in the chief's courtyard. He has some good sized ones."

"You like it here?"

"Of course! I'm glad I came."

"But you can reconsider. Come home with me, Dina, and we'll make a good marriage arrangement for you."

"Now? You want me to exchange caring for Papa in return for running after a man I haven't yet met? Come on, Sol, be sensible!"

He grinned, then said, "All right, you win! Papa would forget to eat if somebody doesn't take care of him. I've never seen anybody like him. . . ."

"Yes, I know. Food and clothes are the least of his worries," she answered. "I think he's something of a saint, Sol."

"A saint? Well, maybe. Anyway, Dina, if you need any money, let me know, and I'll stand by you. But don't ever ask me to live in this godforsaken spot. . . .

"There you go again," the girl said, giggling. "Solomon Marandi, you're funny! How can Khanua be God-forsaken, when he sent us here?"

The young man shrugged, then said with a grin, "You and Papa are two of a kind. I don't understand either of you."

Probably not, for their ears were tuned to another voice, one that commanded their foremost love and loyalty. It cost father and daughter dearly, as it costs anyone who dares to step beyond easy believism into the shoes of discipleship.

One can drown inner heart cries during the busy working hours, but night brings them into distorted proportions. Like a taskmaster demanding answers where there are none, questions kept Benjamin Marandi awake that last night before Sarah left for home. He tossed and turned on his bed out under the stars, a new experience for this man who usually slept with a sense of work well done.

Am I being a good husband, his conscience cried. She says I haven't considered her needs in forcing her to be here with me. Am I so selfish that I visualize her enhancing my work for the Lord rather than seeking those fulfilling dreams of hers? And what sort of a father am I to allow a rift to develop in our family structure?

Benjamin, ever since his conversion, had sought his family's highest interests. And he had brought Sarah here in good faith, hoping she would also hear the Voice and answer the call, even as Bellamdina had done. But Sarah refused to listen. What was his duty? To return with her, considering his former tour as the answer to the call? Should he seek to please Sarah, or was obedience to Jesus Christ imperative?

Not until Benjamin drank deeply of that Gethsemane cup did he sense peace. In the early hours of the morning he fell asleep. When he awoke the hurt remained, but the issue had cleared. Adam had fallen with Eve; through Christ, Benjamin must not follow Sarah, not when she turned away from his Lord's call.

Benjamin and Dina farewelled Sarah and Solomon with many assurances of their love and prayers, but they knew they had come to a turning of the ways. For the remainder of his life, father and daughter spent annual vacations at home with mother and son, but they always returned to continue the ministry to which God had called them.

About a month later, Dulu found Pradhan checking his bow and arrows. "Hi, Pradhan," he said, "you going for a hunt?"

The chief's son looked up from the mat on which he was sitting and said, "Not planning on it. Want to go?"

"Naw . . . " Dulu answered with a grin. "Let's do something different this evening. Come with me to visit Benjamin at the mission."

"Me? What will Dad say?"

"What can he say? We're free men. Benjamin's not forcing us, is he? So let's go! We can listen, and look. How else can we make intelligent decisions?"

"Maybe you're right, but I don't think Dad should know."

They waited until twilight had settled into night, then slipped out under cover of darkness. A small silver moon hung near the horizon, and the stars seemed brighter than usual. A nip in the night air caused the men to draw their cotton shawls closer. Pradhan asked, "Dulu, do you really believe Benjamin was a witch doctor?"

"Why not? When we have the chance we'll test him. If he can

play all the rhythms, fine. Nobody but a witch doctor knows."

"Good idea. What do you think he's up to?"

"Well, I'm curious. I think we'd better check him out."

A flickering light shone from the schoolhouse and Dulu and Pradhan cautiously examined the scene as they drew near.

Kailu and his friend Jatha sat with Benjamin on mats. A lantern hung from a rope on one of the rafters. Near the open book over which the white-haired gentleman bent, the rays of another lantern cast a soft glow.

Benjamin straightened as the two entered. "Dulu! Pradhan! Come, come and join us!" he called. "I'm teaching Jatha and Kailu a new song."

He placed the violin over his left arm, rather than under his chin. Drawing the bow across the strings, Benjamin began to sing, "*Ma añjomtabonpese, Isor kanae Gomke aboren*" (Listen, everybody! God is our great Shepherd). Benjamin sang enthusiastically, and the four novices soon joined in. After repeating the first verse many times, the preacher explained the words.

"See?" he said. "This word, *Isor*, means God. We Santals call him Thakur Jiu."

Pradhan looked up. Did Benjamin Marandi, a Santal, know Thakur Jiu?

"How can Isor be Thakur Jiu?" he asked. "How do you know?"

"Yes, because of who he is," the teacher responded. "Thakur Jiu is the Great Spirit. He's the Good God, and our Creator. Thakur Jiu knows each of us intimately, and holds everything together. Have you heard of him?"

The four pupils nodded and told him of Haram's visit. Then Benjamin continued, "Now, Pradhan, let's answer your question. You're Pradhan, aren't you?"

"Of course."

"But why do they call you Pradhan?" (Pradhan means "leader.")

"Because I'm the chief's son . . . in line for his position. Don't you see the silver stud?"

Benjamin chuckled, then said, "Most surely. But I suppose you're called 'the chief's son' at times? Without the Pradhan?"

"Yes . . . or even 'Raghu's boy' when I visit my grandparents. Makes me feel like I'm about six," he said with a grin, and all laughed.

"Oh, I see," the preacher mused. After a bit the other three young men began to chuckle heartily as Benjamin continued, "Yet you haven't changed? But you have several names?"

The tall, lanky fellow rose and stretched in embarrassment. Soon he began to laugh with the others and said, "You caught me there, didn't you, Benjamin?" When he sat down again he continued, "So God can be Thakur Jiu, or 'Isor' . . . he's one and the same?"

"Right, my boy! Thakur Jiu is the True God. He's also the Good Shepherd, and we can trust him to fully care for us. Now, let's sing our new song once again."

Pradhan and Dulu hummed the catchy little tune with the captivating words over and over again as they walked through the field to the village. Next night they joined Kailu and Jatha, and soon went habitually. In fact, they feared missing their daily music session. Manu, Pradhan's cousin, began to check on his coming and going, but kept the matter to himself. However, the anger that still raged within sought revenge, and Manu thought he might now have the answer.

About the same time, Ram Das Singh, son of the landlord, made it his business to investigate the new family near Khanua.

Chapter Six

Ram Das Investigates the Mission

With the usual music session in full swing, nobody noticed the stocky Brahman youth as he slid into position behind the wall of the empty house on the corner of the new mission compound. In place of the usual white cotton shawl that the villagers used, Ram Das covered his head and body with a dark grey shawl, making it difficult for anyone to determine his identity.

He watched and listened, seeking to capture the intent of the conversation. His knowledge of Santali enabled him to follow easy sentence structures, but he didn't know anything about the religious terminology Benjamin was using.

He was just about to return home when he suddenly noticed another shrouded figure coming his way. Should he run? He decided to wait, and when the person reached the corner of the wall some six feet away from him Ram Das called softly, "Manu, is it you?"

The man started in surprise, then recognized their landlord's son. "Ram Das?" he said, coming over quickly. "What are you doing here?"

"Looks to me like we're doing the same thing," the Brahman whispered. "Who's this white-haired fellow, anyway?"

"He's moved up here from Santal Parganas," Manu said, "and opened this mission."

"Mission?" Ram Das looked startled. "You mean this is a Christian mission?"

"You said it . . . begun by those white Sahibs from Saharsa."

"You don't mean it!" Ram Das looked at his companion in amazement. "Come, I must hear about this. We've seen enough, Manu. Walk home with me."

The two slipped out under cover of darkness and walked the mile to the Singh home. What he heard caused Ram Das to alternate between anger and admiration. To learn those white people had opened a mission under the very noses of their adversaries made the Brahman wonder where they got their power.

He mused, instead of guns, they use kindness; instead of arguments they utilize a Santal of gentle manner, with a violin. And a daughter who's attractive and educated. Hmmm . . . wait until Dad finds out.

Ram Das kept the news to himself, but waited for the right moment to spring the matter on his father, who prided himself in knowing everything about everyone.

Several days later, Khanua's landlord adjusted his gold-rimmed glasses that kept sliding down his nose. He was seated at a small table under the overspreading mango tree in his spacious courtyard. Several well-built brick houses surrounded this open area—his home, three storage houses for grains, and servants' quarters. A pile of hay and millet drying on mats in the far area of the courtyard showed the man to be a gentleman farmer. His attire, however, could have belonged to a politician or college teacher. His sharp features and keen eyes marked him as being astute, one who kept abreast of changing times throughout the world, and informed himself of every detail in his various enterprises.

Now Gopal Singh checked his ledger at the small table under the tree. "Hmmm . . . Kailu owes me forty *rupees*," the man observed with a scowl. "And here's another account—Manu took an advance of two hundred *rupees* to help pay for wedding expenses. That foreman! He's far too lenient with these Santals."

Ram Das looked up from reading the *Patna Weekly* and said, "Foreman? What about you, Dad? When are you going to stop talking and start confiscating land?"

"Watch your words," his father shouted. He swung around, shook a finger at the young fellow and added, "And your manners."

His son laughed. Throwing his paper aside, he stood up and replied, "Dad, you're always grumbling about them. Why do you employ them?"

"Because they're honest, boy! But I can't stand their independence." He paused, then added, "Suppose I get rid of them. Suppose I do—then what?"

"Easy. Plenty more would grab at the chance to work for you."

"Yes? Who?"

"Our kind of people."

"Exactly! Don't be a fool, son. Can't you see we've got it good? Whatever else may be wrong with my sharecroppers, at least they're honest. I can't say that for everyone."

"But you have to pressure them to get your money, Dad. You know that." Ram Das leaned idly against the tree and concluded, "They don't have any sense of time."

The landlord answered absent-mindedly, "No clocks! They run their days by the sun. And no calendars! They just live in their own little world. What do these tribals comprehend of our political changes and upheavals in India?"

"India?" The young man cast his father a sly glance, then queried, "Do you know what's happening in Khanua, Dad?"

"Don't be sassy!"

Ram Das laughed aloud. "We march to Saharsa to finish off the white man. Now he turns around and builds a mission just a mile from us, right under our noses."

Gopal Singh swung around and shouted, "Where?"

"In Khanua."

"Ridiculous!" The landlord leaped up and faced his son. Ram Das guffawed, slapping his knee in mirth. "Ridiculous?" he shouted back. "Dad, it's ridiculous, but true!"

"It can't be," the older man insisted. "If any mission dares to come this direction, I'll know about it."

"Well, they've come," the young Brahman retorted, greatly enjoying his advantage. "Not in the guise you'd expect, however."

"Don't talk nonsense."

"I'm not, Dad," his son said after regaining composure. "You know that new Santal family living near the village? We supposed they own that property, but they don't! The mission in

Saharsa bought it and placed them there. Clever! They don't face us themselves; they send Santals."

"Well, we can't prohibit people buying land, but we'll make life miserable for them if they don't behave themselves," the landlord muttered as he resumed his seat. "But how do you know?" he asked. "Tell me about them."

"I'd like to know more," Ram Das admitted. "Manu gave me my information, but he didn't seem to know much, either. Or perhaps Santals aren't telling all they know. I did learn a few things. Father and daughter live here. The mother and son farm their land in Santal Parganas. The girl's good-looking, Dad. I saw her yesterday when I walked by. She was teaching some children in their schoolhouse."

"Schoolhouse? What schoolhouse?"

"Nothing much . . . just an open shed, with mats spread on the ground."

"How many children?"

"About a dozen, I'd venture." Ram Das idly picked a mango from a low-lying branch and began to peel one end.

"Anything happening yet?"

"I saw the girl's father talking to several men, but he seemed to be holding a music session. I couldn't tell what that was all about, Dad. I'll inquire in Banmankhi tomorrow when I attend the political meeting."

"Good idea, son. Those Christians might be moving this direction. If so, the leaders in Banmankhi will have wind of it." Adjusting his gold-rimmed glasses, Gopal Singh returned to his ledger.

Banmankhi, by far the largest town in the area, lay eleven miles north of Gopal Singh's home. Before dawn the next morning, Ram Das walked four miles to the railway station at Barhara Kothi and caught the train. With several hours to loiter in Banmankhi prior to the meeting, he would have ample time to visit Sohan Lal, known for dispensing gossip. Some called him the local newspaper.

The general store, of which Sohan Lal was the proprietor,

sat conveniently about a block from the station, on the main road. Not only did the store carry a variety of products for home and kitchen, but it acted as a central meeting place for both travelers and townspeople. Several benches underneath the overspreading mango tree in front of the store invited passers-by to come and rest. Ram Das sank down, waiting for Sohan Lal to finish talking to a customer, but before he knew it, he fell asleep. A half-hour later, the shopkeeper's loud voice stirred him into consciousness.

"What's new, Wolie?" he heard the man ask. "You're walking far too fast for this kind of weather."

"You think I know something you don't?"

Ram Das Singh opened his eyes and noted a tall Muslim of genial countenance and alert manner, hair greying around his temples.

"Come on, man," the inquisitive shopkeeper prodded. "Out with it, friend. It's written all over you."

"Well, it's the mission."

The eavesdropper sat bolt upright, then slumped as though sleeping. Wolie stood near the door of the shop, talking to Sohan Lal behind the check-out counter.

"What's new about that? I've known about the mission for a long time—at least two weeks. What's new today?"

"I'm working on the houses, man. Listen, Sohan Lal! One of those adobe houses has a mud floor; the other, a cement one!"

"What? By all the gods—who's going to live there? Is a white Sahib coming to Banmankhi?" The rotund shopkeeper moved from behind the counter to peer at his informant. Coming close he asked confidentially, "Is it one of the white Sahibs I've seen at the station? They always return to Madhipura or Saharsa."

"No, no!" Wolie said with a shake of his head and a big smile. "Neither of those, man. A builder! I've decided to become his apprentice and learn my trade properly."

Ram Das cast a second glance at the tall man. Must be a mason or carpenter, maybe both, he surmised.

Sohan Lal placed his hands on his hips and looked the Muslim in the eye. "Not so fast, Wolie," he warned. "You can't trust these white men. Remember the British?"

"Yes, but these Sahibs are different."

"Well, I'll never trust a Britisher . . . not after the way they grabbed everything for themselves." Sohan Lal turned away and spat, punctuating his disgust.

"Look at you!" the Muslim said with a smile. "How can you forget they gave us our independence? If anything's wrong with India now, Sohan Lal, it's our fault, not theirs. It's our house, isn't it?"

"Nonsense! Who made it the way it was when we took over? The British! There!" The shopkeeper turned back to his work with a "that's finished" look, and Wolie went his way.

Before Sohan Lal could take care of another customer, a neighbor passed. "Come here, Mangu Ram! Come!" he called.

The man stopped, then walked up to the door and said, "What do you want?"

"Have you heard the news?"

"What news?" he asked nonchalantly. "Has the world blown up?"

"Come now, I don't mean politics or Delhi. I'm talking about Banmankhi."

"Banmankhi?" Mangu Ram stopped to pop some *pan* in his mouth before he proceeded. "What happens here? The trains arrive and depart. They take us on our joyrides to Murliganj or Purnea. What else? This place is dead."

Sohan Lal laughed and slapped Mangu Ram on the back as they stood near the door. "Did you eat a green mango for breakfast? Look, friend, I have news for you!"

"All right, spit it out. . . . "

Mangu Ram suited action to his words, spitting the bright red juice of the *pan* leaf he was chewing. The juice, looking like blood, hit the dusty road and evaporated.

"It's the mission, man!" the shopkeeper ejaculated.

"Mission? What's a mission?"

"There's one in Saharsa, on the main bazaar road, near the railway station. You should see that bungalow! People call it the little palace."

"Why?"

"Big house and compound with grassy lawns!" Sohan Lal made a wide sweep of his arms to impress his listener. "White Sahibs live there with their families . . . and listen. . . . "

Sohan's voice dropped to a penetrating whisper, "one of them is moving to our town!"

"Impossible!" Mangu Ram spat again, punctuating his words. "Nobody chooses Banmankhi—not without a good reason." He paused, then added, "But I did see a white man recently in Katihar railway station. I thought the British left. In my opinion, the Sahibs had better stay where they are. Why come to Banmankhi?"

"To make all of us Christians," the shopkeeper muttered as he turned to serve his next customer.

The eavesdropper rose and sauntered off. Ram Das knew he had juicy gossip to share at the political meeting. When he reported Wolie's news, the elders shouted in anger. "We'll boycott the white man! We won't sell him anything in our shops."

With a satisfied smirk, Gopal Singh's son turned homeward, but he walked instead of taking the train. The road led directly south, passing through the large Muslim village of Bishanpur, and fronted the new mission land on which the new houses stood.

"So one has a cement floor," Ram Das muttered. "Wait until my Dad hears this. . . . "

Chapter Seven

Pradhan Learns the Price

Several days later Pradhan stirred before the first streak of dawn tinted the eastern sky. He quietly rose from his rope bed in the courtyard and glanced at Manjli and their two sons still sleeping on bamboo mats. Jatha, aged three, lay face upward with his right arm curled under his head. The baby slept close to his mother.

Pradhan felt an inner surge of excitement as he faced this day. Benjamin Marandi had offered to take him on one of his treks. The chief's son hastily washed his face and hands at the pump, then took care of other chores. When he returned to the house he found Manjli making tea.

"You're up early," she remarked. "Are you going somewhere?" She handed him a glass of the hot, sweet liquid.

"Yes," he answered, "to Barhara Kothi first, where I'll pay our bills. After that, well, I'm not sure how things will work out, but I expect to be home by evening."

He stood, tucked some money into his shirt pocket, put on his sandals, and picked up his umbrella. Before leaving he leaned over and gently touched the baby. The little one stirred, opened his eyes and smiled, then twitched as a fly lit on his nose. "You'd better cover him, Manjli," Pradhan suggested, "or take him indoors. The flies bother him."

She cast her husband a troubled glance. Why his concern? What had happened to her former arrogant husband? Was it his friendship with the newcomer? Though Pradhan didn't share with her concerning his evening sessions, she kept abreast of his movements through his cousin, Manu. Lately Manu had been cultivating the chief again.

Didn't Pradhan realize he jeopardized his position by associating with the preacher? If he kept on, she could foresee trouble.

Unaware of her concern, Pradhan said goodbye and walked briskly through the sleeping village, across the field to the mission compound where Benjamin awaited him.

"*Johar*" (greetings), the young man said, and bowed low before his senior. In response, the former witch doctor touched his left hand to the elbow of his right arm. With his right hand extended he blessed Pradhan in their traditional Santal manner.

"*Johar*," he responded with a smile. "I was looking for you. Bellamdina, bring a cup of tea."

"I've already had one," he said, but nevertheless accepted the tea and plate of puffed rice proffered by Dina. The call of the brainfever bird rent the morning stillness. A white haze clung to the ground, giving the whole a dreamlike quality.

When Pradhan finished eating, Benjamin said, "Come now, it's time to move." He motioned to the east. "It gets hot quickly enough." Benjamin picked up his shoulder bag and violin, and Pradhan carried a large roll of pictures on the life of Christ. The two men started briskly on the footpath that led westward, and in the cool morning air they made good time. Since Pradhan followed the preacher on the narrow foot trails between low-lying rice fields, talking was difficult.

After half an hour, however, they came to open country where they could follow the oxcart road to Barhara Kothi.

"What's your plan, Benjamin?" Pradhan asked.

"To the bazaar first, then directly cross country to Dharkola."

The young man nodded, then queried, "May I stop and pay some bills in Barhara Kothi? I'd like to clear my debts. They have bothered me ever since you said debt drags a person down."

His companion beamed and replied, "Of course we'll stop. Praise God!"

"Where's Dharkola?"

"Near Murliganj."

"Who's there?"

"Patras and Sukul. They're the first Christians in that entire area."

"But what about Tinkonwa, Benjamin? I've heard my father talk about Christians there."

The preacher chuckled, then answered, "Tinkonwa? Christians in Tinkonwa? They're a different brand! Come, let's rest on that log over there, and I'll tell you about them."

Benjamin mopped his brow with the end of his cotton shawl and seated himself, then turned to the young man. "Now, let's see, two kinds of Christians? Oh, yes, . . . have you ever seen a counterfeit *rupee?*"

The young man nodded, and the preacher continued, "You know how to tell the difference? Flip the coin and listen for the ring when it hits the surface."

Pradhan laughed. "What's that got to do with Christians?" he asked.

The elderly man's eyes twinkled as he answered, "A lot, my boy. The true and the counterfeit may look alike, but you may be sure there's no comparison when it comes to value. Put a counterfeit Christian next to a true one. Place both of them in a mess of trouble, and see what happens."

"What happens, Benjamin?"

"One rings true, the other one doesn't."

"How do you mean, rings true?"

Benjamin stood up, stretched, then sat down again. "Let me tell you a story, then you'll understand. Several years ago a missionary from the west came to Tinkonwa and offered our people a free education if they would become Christians. Quite a number thought it a good bargain, so they were baptized and enrolled in the newly opened school."

"And then?"

"They looked for other handouts."

"Like what?"

"Oh, free grains, free housing on the mission compound and jobs."

"But, Benjamin," Pradhan said with a puzzled look, "did they find inner peace, and release from fear?"

"Not the ones I've met, my son. I doubt that any of them personally know the Lord Jesus."

"You mean they haven't changed? I thought Christians trusted in Jesus, not the *bongas.*"

"I hear that many already have returned to *bonga* worship because they became discontented and felt they had been mistreated." The preacher shook his head, then said, "You see,

Pradhan, they didn't change inwardly, so bad habits continued. They like to drink, and then they fight. Tinkonwa doesn't have a very good reputation."

"Oh, Benjamin! And I thought Christians are wonderful people."

"See what you think about Patras and Sukul." The older man stood up and opened his umbrella, which they used to shade themselves from the hot sun as they walked. He said, "Remember, Pradhan, a true Christian has personally met Jesus Christ, and he makes living worthwhile. When you come to him, he transforms you. Your interests change, and new habits replace former ones." It was the first of many such discussions that the two had throughout that day, and Pradhan pushed it back for later use.

Within half an hour, the two Santals reached Barhara Kothi where Pradhan paid his bills. Then they rested ten minutes in a tea shop, and took to the trails again. This time they cut across open fields until they found well-marked oxcart roads leading from village to village.

The men reached Dharkola about noon. When the children saw Benjamin's violin case, they shrilled their welcome, "The music man! The music man has come!" Children ran from everywhere to follow the travelers through the village.

Many of the elders greeted them, but others turned away in anger, muttering, "Traitor! He left *bonga* worship for a foreign religion." But Benjamin walked on undisturbed, a look of peace on his open countenance. He chatted with the children and promised to sing for them.

Near the northern end of the long, drawn-out village, the travelers entered an open courtyard surrounded by several houses. A young man of stocky build looked up from filling bags with grain.

"Benjamin!" he cried. He pushed his straight black hair out of his eyes and quickly rose from his haunches to come forward with outstretched hands. The white-haired preacher laid his umbrella and violin case on a rope bed, then embraced him.

"I've brought Pradhan today," he said, indicating his companion. "And this is Patras, Pradhan."

"Oh, Benjamin, I'm so glad you've come!" Patras exclaimed. "I needed both of you, God knows."

"Shall I call Sukul?" an older boy with sparkling eyes asked. "Yes," Patras answered.

Then turning to Benjamin he said, "Please excuse me while I tell my wife you have come." By the time he returned, the visitors sat on a rope bed surrounded by eager children and their elders. Only the entrance of the young woman bearing a gleaming brass platter and a bowl of water parted the crowd sufficiently to give access to her guests. She washed their feet, bowing low as they accepted her service with the Santal blessing. Patras's wife then retreated to prepare the meal, but first she gave them hot tea with the usual puffed rice.

"Will you stay tonight?" Patras asked.

"Not today," the preacher replied. "I've got to get back. We want to catch the afternoon train from Murliganj."

"Oh! Then we'll have to talk while we eat. The children want a meeting now."

"Yes, yes," they cried. "Tell us stories and sing for us."

The large pictures Pradhan had carried, along with catchy choruses accompanied by Benjamin on his violin, helped the lesson to stick. After the meeting the four men shared deeply together. Much of what the others said seemed strange to Pradhan, but he listened quietly and intently, especially when Patras spoke.

"I'm finding it costs to follow Jesus," Patras remarked. Pradhan thought, then how can you sit there with a smile on your face? It can't be so bad. But Benjamin encouraged Patras by saying, "Tell me about it."

"My brothers threaten to kill me. One of them raised his hand to strike two days ago when I refused to do *bonga* worship. I really thought my end had come, but the Lord saved me. Now the people are calling me a witch, Benjamin. Yesterday they tried to chase me out of the village, but I said I'm serving the Lord God who made heaven and earth. And now today God sent you. See? Isn't he good?"

"You? A witch?" Pradhan asked, incredulous.

Patras nodded and smiled, then continued, "They can't touch me, you know . . . no matter how hard they try. I sense the Lord's protection around me like a wall."

The older man blinked rapidly, then said, "I believe you, my son. I've gone through similar testings, and I've also proved Jesus faithful. You must always stand true. Let me pray for you and Sukul. Strengthen each other. The Lord will bring you through victorious. Don't fear!"

That conversation, along with others that had occurred during this day, impressed Pradhan with having seen and touched a quality of life that rises above circumstance. A thousand thoughts whirled through his mind but he resolutely pushed them back until he was alone that night, at home in Khanua.

Manjli and the children slept, but her husband tossed on his bed out under the stars. Hour after hour he sought the meaning of all he had heard and experienced.

Benjamin's disdain for the *bongas* particularly intrigued Pradhan. You'd think he possessed some secret potion to neutralize Satan's workings, he thought. But the preacher says Jesus is the victor, not potions.

Then his active mind leaped to review Patras's amazing joy in the face of persecution. Where did he find such courage? Would it be available to him also?

Patras's words came back: "It costs to follow Jesus . . . my brothers threaten to kill me . . . I really thought my end had come . . . yesterday they tried to chase me out of the village . . . but I sense the Lord's protection around me like a wall." The words seared Pradhan's soul.

He gazed up at the stars and remembered Benjamin's saying, "The true God lives above the heavens, far above trees or even mountains. He made them all! We must worship him. Turn from evil, Pradhan, and accept the Lord Jesus Christ. The true God is holy, and he desires us to be holy."

But the chief's son felt such action to be impossible. "*Marang Buru* claims us and casts his evil eye upon us," he said aloud. "Who can deliver me from his power?"

A sudden, intense pain gripped the young man in his abdomen. He twisted violently, then stood up to get relief and paced back and forth. A dread thought struck—See? *Marang Buru* is doing this. I've questioned his authority. Is he killing me? "Please, Jesus," Pradhan gasped, "help me . . . Lord! I believe in you."

He suddenly sensed peace, and the young man lay down and slept. Somewhere between consciousness and unconsciousness he dreamed, or was it a vision? No matter! Jesus Christ clearly stood beside his bed and said, "My son, be healed." Pradhan's whole being thrilled with joy so ineffable that he awoke with a start. But the Presence remained, and the Lord's sweet words of assurance and hope replaced the former pain and torment.

Jesus spoke: "I came to deliver you, Pradhan. You don't have to struggle alone. I conquered Satan on the cross, and through me you can win. But you must trust me completely. Will you be mine?"

The young man sat up and said aloud, "Yes, Lord Jesus. I do give myself to you, now! I'm yours, and you are my Lord."

The fountain of joy surged within, accompanied by a peace so exhilarating he felt he was breathing rarified air. Pradhan turned over to sleep, wondering drowsily what his price would be.

Chapter Eight
Khanua Interlude

Some twenty-five miles southwest of Murliganj, in another Santal village, a sick woman huddled on her mat in the corner of her open verandah. Her children, aged eight and two, played in the courtyard. Lukhi burned with fever that she suspected to be the initial stages of smallpox. The sickness had already claimed several lives in the village.

Her husband, Bhima, suddenly rushed into the courtyard with several men urging him on. He towered over his distraught wife and yelled, "You're the witch! You're the witch!" Then he struck blow upon blow in frenzy, using a bamboo stick. Lukhi pled for mercy, but there was none. She cringed and writhed in pain.

"Bhima's wife! Out with her!" the man yelled.

Several women turned to watch and asked, "How do you know?"

"How do we know?" Manjhan bellowed. "Didn't I go with him to the witch doctor? Didn't I hear with my own ears? She's brought this evil thing upon us. Out with her!"

Lukhi arose, and with trembling steps stumbled off the verandah and out of the courtyard onto the village path.

"Go!" the men shouted. "Go . . . and never return if you value your life!"

The stricken woman could scarcely see the path for tears. She managed to reach the shade of a mango tree on the outskirts of the village and sank exhausted to the ground as unconsciousness took over. Her tormenters returned home and said, "There, that's finished. Now we'll have peace."

An hour later Lukhi arose. To whom could she go? Her heart anguished over her children. Who would care for them? But she didn't dare to return. In her confusion an inner voice directed, "Go to Miriam. She'll take you in."

Somehow Lukhi managed to stumble wearily the six miles north. Her incredible journey ended on the doorstep of her former childhood friend, where she sank exhausted. A wan moon shone on the little house near the river.

Miriam looked up from studying her Bible and called, "Who's there?" She opened the door to find a bleeding woman collapsed on the step.

"Oh!" she cried, "it's Lukhi! What's happened to you? Come, let me help." Her loving arms lifted the woman and brought her into the cottage.

"Miriam," Lukhi whispered when she could talk, "I've come. My husband beat me. They say I'm a witch."

"Never mind, dear. Don't talk until you get stronger. I'll take care of you."

"But I think I have smallpox."

"Jesus will cure you. I'll pray."

"Jesus?"

"I'll tell you about him tomorrow. He's wonderful, Lukhi. Now I must clean you up and get you ready to sleep."

Miriam prayed as she worked, and as the sick woman listened she decided this Jesus must hold great power over both sickness and evil. Lukhi's eyes followed her friend's every movement, noting the fine, delicate features of her face set aglow with an inner light. What made Miriam so kind and loving? Well, she'd find out tomorrow. Lukhi, too drowsy to follow the matter now, turned over and slept.

But the next day she asked, "Where's your family?"

"My husband left me for another woman when I became a Christian, and my son, Robin, has gone to boarding school," Miriam replied softly.

"Oh," Lukhi whispered, her eyes filling with tears, "I didn't know. I'm sorry. So you've suffered, too. . . . "

"Yes, Lukhi, I know."

"I want my children so badly . . . I can hardly stand it," the woman sobbed. "What's happening to them?"

"Let's ask the Lord Jesus to care for them," Miriam answered.

That led to many witnessing sessions, and soon Miriam's loving service brought Lukhi back to health, and into a living faith. She requested baptism and chose Martha as her name.

Martha's aptitude for housework released Miriam to witness in nearby villages, a work she dearly loved. But the woman faced much opposition, and soon malicious rumors began to circulate about the two women who lived in the house by the river. About six months after Dina's mother returned to Santal Parganas, the mission authorities moved Miriam and Martha to the unoccupied house on the Khanua compound. Dina rejoiced!

They had just concluded their morning worship when they heard Dina calling, "Miriam, Martha! Look here!" They hurried out to see Benjamin's daughter waving a letter. "Look here," she exclaimed.

"What is it?"

"Two missionary ladies are coming for a month's tour to Khanua. Khanua, mind you! They arrive next Monday evening from Banmankhi."

"You mean Saharsa?" Miriam asked.

"No, it's the Memsahibs from Madhipura and Banmankhi."

Miriam looked perplexed. "The Dick Memsahib? I heard she now lives in Madhipura? They moved from Saharsa?"

"Yes," Dina said with a wide smile.

"It's too hot for tents," Miriam added.

"No, no," Dina said emphatically, "they mustn't live in tents. We'll give them our house. My father will move to the school, and I'll use the storeroom. See? We'll vacate gladly for the ladies. They'll be comfortable there."

With daily temperatures soaring over the one hundred degree mark, their concern was justified.

About four o'clock that afternoon, the distant sound of a motorcycle broke the stillness. Soon a white man and little girl rode into view. Curious bystanders followed the visitors through the village, across the field on the path over to the mission. There the Sahib brought his strange vehicle to a halt in front of the schoolhouse. Benjamin, Dina, and the other two ladies came running. The villagers crowded around the newcomers.

"*Johar*, Benjamin," the foreigner said. He removed his pith helmet and mopped his brow. His grey eyes twinkled as he saw the astonishment the motorcycle caused, and the villagers murmured approval when they noted his black hair, alert manner and lithe figure. The ladies whispered, "He brought a *pakku* (little one) with him!"

"*Johar*," Pastor Benjamin responded, then pointed to the motorcycle and asked, "What is it?" To everyone's laughter came the observation by one villager, "It says 'phut-phut-phut.' It's a 'phut-phutia' of course!"

And thus it became.

The missionary lifted his brown-haired, brown-eyed, four-year-old off and placed her beside Dina who began talking to her in Hindi. With the motorcycle and little girl breaking barriers, the Santals quickly accepted the new Sahib Allen Buckwalter and his daughter. Joanne was called "Pakku" from the first day, and the motorcycle the "phut-phutia." Both became an integral part of the Khanua scene, and both were prime favorites!

After the initial pleasantries on that hot afternoon in March, Benjamin and Dina gave their visitors tea. Benjamin asked, "Sahib Ji, can you buy food?"

"Yes, of course." The missionary laughed, then inquired, "Did you think we couldn't?"

"Our landlord's son, Ram Das Singh, said all the shopkeepers are boycotting you."

"Not that I've noticed, Benjamin. In fact, when we arrived several weeks ago by train, almost thirty people escorted Joanne's mother to her new home while Joanne and I rode the mile on our motorcycle.

"That's interesting!" the preacher exclaimed.

"Yes, Joanne's baby doll won them."

Joanne looked up and asked, "Shall I tell him, Daddy?"

"Yes, sweetheart," he answered.

"Her name's Shirley," she began in clear Hindi. "She says 'Mama,' and sleeps—so I think she's special. And she looks like a real baby. My mommy made her a red jacket, and a skirt and hat for Christmas."

"So you brought your dollie to Banmankhi?" the preacher prompted.

The girl nodded, then said, "When we got off the train, I asked Mommy to carry her since I rode with Daddy on the motorcycle and I didn't want Shirley to get dusty."

Dina asked, "What do people think of your dollie?"

"Oh, they want to touch her. Now I show her to everybody."

"Will you bring her here? We'd like to see her, too."

The little white-faced, brown-haired girl shook her head. "No," she said, "the motorcycle is too jiggly. But when you come to see me, I'll show her."

"We'll come, Pakku, yes, we'll come!" Dina replied.

"Did you receive my letter, Benjamin?" the missionary asked.

"Yes, yes, we're looking for the ladies on Monday evening."

Dina spoke up, "We think it's too hot for tents, so my father and I will give them this house."

"And what will you do?"

"We'll manage," she replied, and her father nodded.

"Then we'll be on our way. I'd like to get home before dark."

By late Monday afternoon the villagers spotted two oxcarts lumbering toward Khanua on the dusty road from Banmankhi. They spread the news. "They've come! They've come!"

"Is Pakku with them?"

"No, I don't think so," Miriam answered. She stood with a group of women on the banks of the stream that separated the village from the main road. As they watched the oxcarts approach, Dukua's wife asked, "Why isn't Pakku coming?" Clearly, the little white girl had already won their hearts.

Miriam answered with a big smile, "She will, every weekend, when her father brings her on his motorcycle."

"How long are the ladies staying?"

"A full month, until the new moon shines again!"

"But what will they do here?"

"They're visiting us. The older woman lives in Madhipura, and the younger one has just moved to Banmankhi. We must be good to them. They're our guests!"

The women nodded and joined Miriam as she hurried forward to greet the ladies.

On one pretext or another, almost every Santal in Khanua

village managed to visit the mission by nightfall. They wandered freely, touching the cots and tables in the cottage. They laughed at the cute way the chairs folded up when they tried to sit on them. They examined the aluminum plates and cutlery, all neatly arranged in a small cupboard, and asked the white ladies in their broken Hindi, "Are all these things yours?"

"Oh, Aunt Nellie!" the auburn-haired missionary whispered, "I'm ashamed. What would they say if they saw the Saharsa bungalow?"

"We belong to two different cultures. It's only natural."

"But how can we ever hope to relate until we come to their level?" she asked.

"Don't worry, Leoda. The Lord will bridge the gap."

The younger woman wanted to answer, but kept quiet. She thought, I'm glad I'm wearing *saris* instead of dresses. At least they know I'm not a man!

Behind her decision to change from western garb to *saris* were months of inner struggle. All during her first term, she had worn dresses, as did the other missionary ladies. But when she learned that she would be living in an area where the term "mission" was yet unknown, where no other white woman had lived, this daughter of missionary parents felt it time for another change in lifestyle. When it lay within her power to clear doubts as to who she was, wouldn't the Lord hold her answerable if she desisted?

So Leoda laid aside dresses, and wore *saris* from the day she arrived in Banmankhi. Her husband asked, rather amused, "Which Indian woman are you trying to imitate?"

"One of my educational level," she replied, and from that day onward took a lady doctor as her norm for behavior patterns. And although her decision was not understood by the other lady missionaries, they began to view the *sari* much more favorably from then onward, and later came to adopt its usage much more widely than during the twenty-five years that preceded this.

Most certainly, it was easier for the villagers in Khanua to accept Joanne's mother in her Indian role than it would have been otherwise.

That month of living among the Santals taught the missionary ladies much. The first lesson came the night of their arrival, when the village women asked them, "Are all these things yours?"

The second lesson followed hard on the first. Weary from their cart ride over dusty trails, the missionaries longed for a good night's rest. They had made their cots, and surely tomorrow morning would be adequate time for them to appear on duty.

Yet how could they disappoint Pastor Benjamin and Dina and the others when they expected the ladies to join for evening prayers? This would follow their meal!

So they partook of the delicious curry and rice that Dina had prepared. She served them, talking and laughing with the sheer joy of their presence. And even as they gave themselves to being everything these lonely Christians needed, they found the long evening hours passing in the midst of those few who had struggled on alone.

It was midnight when two weary missionaries finally went to bed, but they set the alarm so that they would awaken in time for morning prayers!

Morning prayers had just concluded when Joanne's mother turned to Benjamin and asked, "Could we have some time together each noon?"

The white-haired preacher blinked in surprise, then said, "Why, yes, Memsahib. Of course. I'll arrange by doing my visiting and shopping in the mornings. That will free me for the rest of the day. What do you have in mind?"

"Village meetings every evening, Pastor," she replied. "And do you think my accordion and your violin would go together?"

He slapped his knee enthusiastically. "Yes, yes," he cried. "I've heard about your foreign instrument but I've never seen one. Did you bring it?"

She laughed softly, then said, "Yes, I'll get it for you." The Santals followed her like eager children and awaited her on the verandah of the big house, so she gave them a ten minute recital of Indian lyrics she had learned from missionary parents in her formative years, and used all through her first term.

"More! More!" they requested, laughing with abandon.

"Not now," she replied, "but you may tell everyone that Pastor Benjamin and I will play our instruments this evening over in the village commons."

The crowd dispersed. Dina turned back to the schoolhouse

to prepare for the children. Mrs. Dick and Miriam started over to the village to begin visitation. Martha hurried off to cook her best curry for the guests, and Benjamin turned to the Banmankhi Memsahib and asked, "May we continue our talk now? I'm curious to know your plans for the month."

"Yes, Pastor Benjamin," she replied. "Please come in."

A large hibiscus bush with beautiful red flowers caught her eye. Leoda walked over and plucked a blossom, then led the way into the one-roomed house that now served as headquarters for this Khanua tour. "Please be seated," she invited the preacher, and took the other chair at the small table that served so many purposes.

"You have beautiful flowers," she began, as she held it toward him. "What you see is the flower, isn't it?"

He nodded, and she continued, "But it's held up by a stem?"

He looked perplexed, wondering where this was leading, but answered, "Of course."

"Well, you and Dina, Miriam, and Martha are the flower," Joanne's mother replied. "Mrs. Dick and I are the stem." She spoke in fluent Hindi, but already had noticed how difficult it was to communicate with those who used another language. So she said thoughtfully, "Pastor, I've come to try something new. For the past twenty-five years, whenever missionaries have gone out on evangelistic tours, they have been in the forefront. But the Lord is telling me it's time for the foreign missionary to fade into the background and yet help in any way possible. Would you be willing to accept Mrs. Dick and me into your team?"

"Which one of you will preach? The Dick Memsahib or you?"

The missionary laughed, then said, "You're the preacher!"

"But it's your tour," he remonstrated.

"And your people!" She pulled her chair close, then continued, "Pastor, our Hindi won't go very far. You know that."

"I'll interpret for you."

"Thanks, but we really want you to preach every evening. I'll get the lessons ready each morning. That's why I asked whether we can meet regularly at noon. You'll need time to study and pray on your own in the afternoons while Dina and I visit in the village."

"Oh, I see!" His eyes began to gleam. "It's our meeting!"

"Exactly!" Leoda laughed, then said, "I'm here to help. I've brought flannelgraph pictures to illustrate the life of Christ. As you preach, I'll put them on the board, and together we'll give the village a concentrated month of teaching. We're praying that someone will find courage to step out publicly for Jesus Christ."

The converted witch doctor wiped his misty eyes. "I've preached for almost a year," he said, "but nobody has yet done that."

"It's not wasted effort, Pastor. You've laid a good foundation. Now, by the grace of God, we'll pray for decision. Are you agreed?"

"Memsahib," he said blinking hard, "I'm glad to know I'm not alone."

"Well, the Lord sent me, so I know he's planning something special for Khanua."

"Oh, Memsahib!"

She sat quietly for a little, then spoke softly, "You worked with my husband in that other tour, Benjamin. Now you and I have a chance to work together, but this will be different than when the Sahibs were with you. Do you mind?"

"You're more than helpers!" the white-haired gentleman exclaimed. "You've been sent of God to give us hope!"

Neither could foresee what the Lord would do, but that quiet moment of prayer and planning forged a unity of spirit that continued through six years of missionary endeavor, during which time a church was birthed.

Chapter Nine

Jatha's Courage

Khanua village had never before experienced such a meeting. As darkness fell, shrouded figures moved silently toward the village commons, near the chief's home. A bright gas lamp hung from a tree, lighting up the flannelgraph board. A rope bed and several wooden chairs completed the arrangements.

The two musicians took their places in front while the other team members clustered around the bed. With the violin and accordion leading, young men and children sang the lyrics they had learned from Benjamin and Dina. Then Benjamin preached.

Dukua, one of Gopal Singh's tenants, determined to tell Ram Das about it. As he measured out grains next day under the young Brahman's watchful eye, he stopped long enough to say casually, "Two white women have come."

"White women? You mean white men."

"No, not men. White women," the Santal repeated with a broad smile. "They're staying at the mission for one month."

"Women? What are they doing?"

"What can a woman do? Nothing!" Dukua spat on the ground, singularly enjoying his advantage over this young man who always prided himself on keeping abreast of the news.

"Well?" prompted Ram Das.

"The younger one doesn't have black hair. It's reddish brown, like the Moslems when they return from visiting their holy place. Where is it?"

"Mecca," the young man said with a broad grin.

"Well, wherever it is," Dukua acknowledged, and added, "No matter to me. . . . The older white woman comes from Madhipura."

"And the younger?"

"Banmankhi."

"Banmankhi?" Ram Das looked startled. "Are they from the mission?"

"Yes, of course. What other white people live here? The British left."

"Hold your tongue and manners!" Ram Das said, giving the bag of grain a kick just to vent his feelings. Some spilled out, and Dukua leaned over and swept the grain together, then restored it without comment. Ram Das watched him, then said, "On second thought, I'm glad you told me about your guests. Perhaps my father and I could invite them here for tea. I'd like to meet them."

"You could attend the meeting each evening," the Santal suggested slyly. "You understand enough Santali to follow."

"What meetings?"

"Oh, it's grand. There's music and pictures, while the preacher talks. He tells interesting stories, so that we can easily follow. And you'd like the music. Benjamin plays his instrument while one of the ladies accompanies on hers."

"What is hers like?"

"It's foreign, sort of like a harmonium, except that she wears it on her chest with straps holding it. She pumps with her other hand while playing it . . . no, that's not quite right. I don't know how to explain it. You'll just have to come and see."

"No, thank you," Ram Das muttered. "I'm not interested."

Dukua shrugged his shoulders, picked up his basket of grain and turned homeward. A hint of a smile and a twinkle in his eyes suggested he felt he had done very well. In fact, he decided to watch for Ram Das that evening. The preacher's sermon would be good for that upstart, he concluded.

As the sounds of music wafted over the evening air, the people began to gather. Men sat on their haunches, as usual, their sheets drawn around their heads and shoulders, to all but hide their faces. The women stood or sat in the back, similarly shrouded. Several lepers, brothers, sat off to one side.

Dukua watched the footpath from Gopal Singh's house and grinned when a lone figure slipped around the back of a hut to join the group.

Thought it would work, he mused. Give it to him, Benjamin!

Ram Das managed to attend every meeting, sometimes

lying to his father to keep him from learning his interest. He had read portions of the Bible during his college courses in world literature, but this was the first time he heard the story of Jesus consecutively. Aided by the flannelgraph illustrations, he managed to follow each message. Initially, curiosity drew Ram Das Singh, but interest held him. His former antipathy to the Christians and their message changed to alarm when he began to see himself in the light of God's holiness. Now the proud young Brahman wished he could read the Bible for himself.

Each message strengthened the impact made the former night. Throughout the three weeks Benjamin's listeners found themselves faced with a choice they preferred not to make. Pradhan, in particular, labored under a sense of foreboding, something sinister. He wanted to identify with the Christians. He knew his heart belonged to Jesus, but he couldn't step out to make public declaration. At least, not yet.

Jatha, small in stature but stalwart in character, had no such qualms. As charter member of the music class Jatha sang lustily every night. He sat close to the rope bed, right at the heart of the action, and listened carefully to every message. He helped wherever needed, showing from the very first where his sympathies lay. And at the conclusion of the third week Jatha knew his hour had come. It was Palm Sunday weekend.

On Saturday afternoon the Banmankhi Sahib and his brown-haired daughter arrived by motorcycle. As the team lingered over their tea and snacks, Benjamin said, "Sahib Ji, may I go to Jhungi village tomorrow? Paul, the leper, is the only Christian in the area. He mustn't feel we've forgotten him."

"Of course, Benjamin. It's only right that you go. We'll manage. I'll preach in Hindi, and Dina can interpret."

Benjamin nodded, and with misty eyes continued, "Many of our Khanua folks are now considering becoming Christians . . . Dukua among them."

"Pradhan?" the Dick Memsahib asked.

"Not yet. The chief and Pradhan's wife are fighting him. They're afraid he'll take a stand. I think he's waiting for other members of his family."

"But he and Dulu come regularly every day. We used to

think Guru would be the first to break through, but now he's slipped behind. Isn't it true, Papa?" Dina added.

"Perhaps Manu has something to do with that," Benjamin replied. "I feel he's stiffening."

"Well," the Sahib began, "how about giving another full week of teaching, then plan a baptismal service for Easter? Don't you think that would be a good day for new beginnings?"

Benjamin laughed, wiping his misty eyes at the same time. "Easter?" he answered. "That's perfect! I'll tell them it celebrates Christ's resurrection from the dead."

Next morning, Palm Sunday, Benjamin left early for Jhungi village. Word spread through Khanua that the Banmankhi Sahib would preach, so a goodly number of villagers found one excuse or another to wander over to the mission about church time. The schoolhouse overflowed.

Jatha sat unnoticed among the others and stayed throughout the day. About four in the afternoon he approached Miriam. "I believe in Jesus," he said. "I want to be baptized today."

She blinked in surprise. "Wait until Pastor Benjamin comes," she advised. "He'll be home tonight."

"Too late," he muttered and shook his head. "I promised the Lord Jesus I'd follow him in baptism today."

"Well, let me ask Dina."

Dina and the missionaries thought Jatha should wait until Easter, but the young man became even more insistent. "Come," he said, pulling at Miriam's shawl. "Today is my day! Come, before the sun sets. My father's gone away today, so I'm free. Come. . . . "

"Wait until next Sunday," Miriam admonished.

"Look!" he said, "My father can't stop me, but you can. I've already moved my clothes and belongings into the oxshed at home. I've spread my mat for tonight. I expect to be baptized today. My family may kill me, but I don't care! I've promised the Lord Jesus to obey him and be baptized today."

"What do you say, Aunt Nellie?" the Sahib asked his senior.

"He's very insistent. . . . I suppose we ought to honor his request."

"What do you say, Leoda?"

"We have a precedent in Scripture, Allen. What about the Ethiopian eunuch?"

He grinned, then chuckled, "Come on, all of you, let's go!"

"Praise God!" Jatha exulted. He would have been bypassed in any search for leadership, yet he knew when his hour came, and he fearlessly led the small band of Christians to the stream on the opposite side of the village.

"Where are you going?" the onlookers asked. "Isn't there any meeting tonight?"

"No meeting," Miriam answered, "but a baptismal service at the stream. Jatha Murmu requests baptism."

"Jatha?"

Shocked neighbors spread the word and streams of people joined the band of singing Christians. Everyone wanted to witness this event. They may not have understood its implications, but they surely sensed its importance, and many wished they possessed the young man's courage.

Everyone had sat incognito in the darkness to hear Benjamin preach. But Jatha was now breaking openly with *bonga* worship, and his action affected the total community. In fact, he was splintering it into fragments! Who could foresee its far-reaching results?

"Jatha," the missionary asked clearly as the two of them stood near the water, "are you willing to tell your people about your faith in Jesus Christ?"

"Yes, Sahib Ji." The young man faced his silent spectators. "Nobody has forced me to follow Jesus," he said. "I sat among you each night and listened, even as all of you have done. And I've learned to read, so I know that Pastor Benjamin is preaching the Word of God. I have given myself to Jesus Christ. I know he is greater than Satan and the evil spirits. I forsake *bonga* worship! Now I trust my Lord to take care of me, and I've promised to follow him in baptism today."

"Ah. . . . " the crowd murmured, as the Christians began to sing in Santali, "I have decided to follow Jesus. . . . No turning back, no turning back."

The missionary stepped into the stream, now barely more than a mudhole. Jatha followed, and the crowd pushed to see as the missionary baptized him, changing his name to Daniel and his status irrevocably.

With the sun hovering near the horizon, the little band of Christians returned to the mission. All remained quiet in the village until the sound of the motorcycle bearing the Sahib and his daughter faded into the distance. Then bedlam broke loose in Khanua.

Chapter Ten

The Council Convenes

When Benjamin returned home that night, he heard the beating of the drums, and knew from the rhythms that the villagers were seeking to appease the evil spirits. He blinked in astonishment and asked Bellamdina, "What happened, daughter?"

"Jatha was baptized this evening, Papa," she announced with a broad smile. "He's Daniel now."

"But why didn't he wait until next Sunday?"

"We tried our best, Papa, but he insisted on today."

The preacher smiled, then said, "Yes, I know. We Santals are peculiar in that respect. We want to choose our own time. It's our independent spirit. I did the same. So Jatha has been baptized. . . . "

Dina handed her father a cup of hot tea as he sat in the schoolhouse. She presumed the missionaries had gone to bed since all was dark in their quarters.

The drums continued throughout the night, and in the early morning scores of villagers left for the witch doctor to sacrifice to *Marang Buru* and the *bongas*. A pall of impending disaster settled over Khanua, yet within many houses new believers prayed for Jatha who dared cause this disruption by following Jesus Christ. "Give us like courage," they cried.

Gopal Singh heard the news by Monday noon. He yelled, "Does anyone dare to become a Christian? He forfeits his land." Interestingly enough, Ram Das waited until his father's anger cooled, then said, "Dad, you're known for your fairness."

"Yes, young man?"

"How can you confiscate land from a family whose grown son becomes a Christian? The father isn't responsible."

Gopal Singh glared at Ram Das as they stood together

under the mango tree. "What's happened to you?" he snapped. "I thought you hated Christians."

"I'm talking about being fair, Dad."

His father grunted and walked off, and the young man smiled.

In Raghu's courtyard, battle lines became more clear. Manu began to needle his uncle with confidence, saying, "See? The Christians are getting stronger. You'd better watch Pradhan. He's pretty friendly with that gang, so you know what will happen."

It hurt, because Raghu knew it to be true. Yet try as he would, he hated the thought of replacing Pradhan with Manu, if and when the village needed a new chief. So Pradhan's father shouted, "If anyone goes to the mission compound, they're in line for excommunication!" The boys snickered, and the chief heightened his vigilance, choosing Manjli, his daughter-in-law, as his main ally. He called her on Monday morning. She looked up from spreading grains to dry on mats under the hot sun, then came over to Raghu sitting under the mango tree, making rope. "Yes, sir?" she said demurely with a low bow.

"I want you to watch your husband for me, daughter. Manu is out to get him, and my son is so naive, he doesn't realize it. We must protect him, for his own good. Do you see?"

She stood erect and answered, "Yes, sir. Since the preacher came, he's changed a great deal . . . almost as though he's mesmerized. I'm sure he goes there every evening instead of meeting others his own age here in the village."

"Well, do what you can to break that infernal friendship! Likely, since I've threatened to excommunicate anyone visiting the mission compound, he'll be more careful. Basically, Pradhan's a good boy."

Raghu dismissed Manjli with a wave of his hand, and she turned to complete her task. But turmoil raged within and her thoughts shouted . . . if Pradhan continues, he'll lose his position. Where does that put me?

The young woman kicked the grain with her bare feet as she spread it on the mat. It helped vent her feelings.

The thought continued. What chance have I of stopping him when young men go off on their own every evening? Why has the chief bound me to watch my husband? Why doesn't he do it himself? Several more vengeful kicks helped!

About that time her mother-in-law came out and yelled, "You're taking your time, girl! Don't you know we have a lot of work to do?"

Her anger flared, but she didn't dare answer back. She'd like to tell her off, she would!

With resentment building and pressure mounting throughout the day, Manjli let it burst forth that evening when her husband came in from the fields. She entered the bedroom and cried, "For once, Pradhan, think of your family and not just yourself."

He looked at her in amazement. "What's happened, love?" he asked quietly.

"All your sweet words!" she snapped. "Don't you know your friendship with that white-haired preacher is getting both of us into trouble? If you really love me, why don't you stop seeing him? Manu's got you where he wants you—and that means your position is jeopardized."

"I suppose you're talking about all the hullabaloo in the village, Manjli? Why blame the preacher? He wasn't even here when Jatha requested baptism. And Jatha made it absolutely clear that nobody pressured him. He's an adult. He can decide for himself, so why all the fuss?"

"I don't know," she said as she sat down weakly. "All I know is that I've had a terrible day with your father and mother both after me. For my sake, Pradhan, please stay away from that preacher so that this household quiets down."

She heard her mother-in-law call, and dashed out the door into the courtyard. "Yes, I'm coming," she answered.

Pradhan felt completely deflated. Out in the field he had spent much time praying, asking for courage to stand in the face of Manu's cutting words. But Manjli? Did she hurt him deliberately?

How could he stop meeting with the Christians when his heart belonged to Jesus Christ? How could he? The daily fellowship and prayer support had become his lifeline! Pradhan stared numbly at the door and wondered what to do.

Out in that *manjhithan* the elders continued their deliberations. As the chief's son glanced in their direction his own spirits began to lift. He grinned and thought, at least I'm not sitting there in the midst of that pressure. He resolved to go and visit Jatha.

Jatha, now Daniel, looked up with a smile as the young man neared the oxshed. "You coming to see me?" he questioned.

Pradhan nodded, then squatted on the mat and said, "Might as well take my stand. I sure admired you taking yours! I wish I had your courage."

"But you do have courage, Pradhan. When it's your day, you'll know. I knew when mine came . . . no doubting it."

"Did you know Dad's threatened to excommunicate anyone who goes over to the mission?"

Daniel shook his head affirmatively, then answered, "Yes, Mom told me. Dad won't even talk to me, but she does . . . and last night she brought me enough food for all day. She believes, you know."

"She does? Man, that's wonderful!" The chief's son slapped Daniel on the back. He suddenly realized that his sense of being trapped had lifted. He was no longer alone! The two young men prayed together, and Pradhan determined he must see Benjamin that very night.

Several hours later, after eating his food, Pradhan slipped over to Dulu's house. "Tired?" he asked as they walked out under the stars.

"Rather! What a day! We're evenly divided, you know."

"Who's there?"

"Everybody but you. They suspect you, of course, so you're out. Funny thing, buddy. They let me sit among them, and Kailu. In fact, at least half of the council members are on our side."

"You don't say! Hey, man! That's better than I expected. When Dad told me I couldn't come, I felt sort of left out, but maybe there's more good in this than I thought. . . ." Pradhan grinned, and Dulu chuckled.

"Say that again," he answered. "For one thing, we know where Manu is when council's in session, and be sure I'm all ears when he talks."

"Manu? He cut me down last night, but I don't care. What hurts more is Manjli's asking me not to see Benjamin again. But I can't listen to her, Dulu. I can't!"

"You telling me? You and I are working under higher orders than hers. Keep right on going over there, buddy. I'll supply you with information to pass on. How will Benjamin find out otherwise?"

"You coming with me?"

"Not tonight, nor as long as council deliberates Jatha's case. I don't want to jeopardize my seat. But I'm counting on you, Pradhan. Right?"

"Right," and their eyes met in an understanding pact. With a slight nod and smile, Pradhan stole out into the night.

Five minutes later Pastor Benjamin heard a familiar voice calling softly from the shadows, "Pastor . . . Pastor Benjamin."

"Pradhan! Where are you?"

"Under the window."

"Come inside quickly, boy."

The young man jumped onto the verandah, and the door opened sufficiently for him to enter, then closed again. He and the pastor embraced each other, then joined the five ladies seated on mats.

"You're having evening prayers?" Pradhan queried.

"We've been praying for you and the others. The schoolhouse seemed very quiet tonight when nobody came for music class."

Pradhan chuckled, "Well, life is interesting in the village right now. My Dad's threatened to excommunicate anyone who comes to the mission."

"Is he now?" the preacher said in amazement. "I tried to go over this evening, but some of your brothers yelled, 'Go back! Go back!' So I thought I'd better wait for further word from you before making matters worse by my presence."

"Don't come over, Pastor. I'll come here instead and keep you informed."

"But what happens if your father finds out?" Mrs. Dick asked.

"At the best, excommunication perhaps, and at the worst, they could poison my food," the young man said with a smile. "My wife does the cooking, you know."

"What has happened to Jatha, I mean Daniel?" Dina asked.

"I found him in the oxshed this evening, enjoying reading his

Bible. He's doing fine and sends his love to all of you."

"Has he had any food, Pradhan?"

"And what happened when his father returned last night?"

"Oh, a big fuss! His dad disowned him . . . forbade anyone to give him food, but his mother just waited until about midnight, then took enough for all of today, too!"

"You don't say!" The pastor blinked rapidly, then wiped his misty eyes.

"He says his mom believes."

"Well, praise the Lord!"

"What about the council? Are they meeting? Why aren't you in it . . . or are you?"

"Manu tattled on me, Pastor. He told my dad I've been coming over here regularly, so Dad lost his temper. He told me I didn't dare sit on the council, that I would be prejudiced. Yes, they've been in session since early afternoon, until about an hour ago."

"Any decisions?" Mrs. Dick asked.

Pradhan laughed, then answered, "Nothing yet. Dulu says they're neatly divided down the middle, for and against Jatha, I mean Daniel."

The preacher thought deeply, then said, "In that case this may drag on for days."

The chief's son stood up and stretched, then said, "You're right, Pastor. I'd better be going now, but I'll come again—likely late at night, and to the schoolhouse."

"Great! I'll be looking for you, Pradhan."

After a heartwarming prayer the young man slipped out again into the darkness.

He came over the next night and called softly. Benjamin sat up, then motioned him to sit on the bed. In the darkness, Pradhan passed on the messages that both Dulu and Daniel had sent, then continued by saying, "We're praying together, Daniel and I, when the council is in session."

Benjamin commented, "I'm proud of both of you, and so is the Lord."

"But Daniel's stepped out, and I haven't."

"Never mind, son. You're very helpful to us right now. By

the way, the Dick Memsahib returned to Madhipura today."

"Why?"

"To get ready for Easter, she said."

"And Joanne's mother?"

"She's here, and a big help to Dina right now . . . in fact, to all of us."

"That's good, Pastor. We need each other."

"Yes, my boy."

The village council battled throughout the entire week. On Good Friday, Benjamin's joy overflowed as he preached to the small group assembled in the parsonage. "Isn't God good?" he asked. "We don't have to work up to victory. Our Jesus won it on the cross! He conquered Satan on the cross! So, all this week we have rested in that victory and enjoyed fellowship with each other." He wiped his misty eyes, then asked the missionary, "Do you know what the battle's all about, Memsahib?"

"Well, I heard they're trying to decide Daniel's fate," she said.

He laughed, then replied, "The one side is asking the other, 'How can you throw out someone who's already left of his own choosing?' "

"They're clever! No wonder it's taking all week to find the answer."

"By the way, Memsahib, why didn't the Sahib come today?" Dina inquired. "I wondered what would happen if he drove through the village."

"No, Dina, he knows. Mrs. Dick stopped at the mission on her way to Madhipura and gave him an update. I've received a note from my husband saying he's not coming until I send further word."

She had barely finished speaking when Pradhan burst in. Eyes shining, he exclaimed, "I told you! The Lord won!"

"What do you mean?" Benjamin asked. Everyone crowded around to hear and he answered, "Dulu told me as soon as he could. I ditched my work in the field to come and report."

"What, Pradhan?"

"The verdict? Listen! 'We cannot excommunicate Jatha. He has voluntarily chosen to become a Christian. He is free to do so and remains a member of the Santal community.' "

Miriam danced for joy while Dina and Martha wept quietly. Benjamin raised both hands in worship, tears streaming down his cheeks. Leoda remarked softly, even while wiping her moist eyes with her handkerchief, "Pastor, this is a new day. Daniel forced the decision by staying in his home after taking baptism. This is good."

"Patras did it in Dharkola," Benjamin remarked, "and now, Daniel."

"The church has taken root. It will grow. It is God's doings!"

He turned to her with radiant face and affirmed, "Praise God forever! All we had to do was trust."

The missionary pushed back an auburn lock. She had really missed her husband and daughter during these strenuous waiting days. Now she felt released, so asked Benjamin, "May I go home tomorrow? I feel I've finished my work here, at least for this time. Do you mind my spending Easter with my husband and daughter?"

He blinked rapidly, then answered, "Yes, Memsahib, you go. Thank you for staying with us. You have made the week much easier for everybody."

"It's been my privilege, and I've learned so much! Thank you for taking me in."

She returned to Banmankhi on Saturday, anticipating a quiet weekend. In Khanua, Benjamin wondered who would attend the Easter service. Would anybody have the courage to break the chief's threat of excommunication?

Instead of fear, those whose hearts were already toward the Lord came to the service, including Dulu and Pradhan. Even Manu, for reasons of his own, came in late and sat in the back.

But just prior to the service, Paul's wife and daughter from Jhungi village arrived. They approached Benjamin and said, "We believe, Pastor. After you left us last Sunday we prayed and asked the Lord to come into our lives. Now we want to be baptized today."

Benjamin blinked rapidly, then replied, "I don't believe the Banmankhi Sahib is coming today."

"I'll take a message," Pradhan offered.

"Good! I'll write a quick note. Sorry you have to miss service, Pradhan, but this, too, is important."

In midafternoon, Pradhan walked up to the grass house with the cement floor and found the missionary family enjoying tea and snacks under a shade tree. They looked up in surprise and welcomed him.

"What is it?" the Sahib asked.

"An urgent note from Pastor," the young man replied. A quick reading brought forth a whistle of astonishment from the missionary. His wife asked, "Is something wrong?"

"It's very all right," he said, rising. "Where's my motorcycle? Come on, Pradhan. Two people have come from Jhungi and desire baptism today."

For Pradhan this was his first experience on the "phut-phutia." He patted disappointed Joanne on the head and said kindly, "Do you mind, Pakku? I'm taking your seat?"

She smiled and replied, "I hope you like it as much as I do. I'll go next time."

In truth, his first five minutes seemed scary. Clinging on desperately, he learned to balance and sway, and by the time they reached Khanua he was riding confidently. In fact, as they motored the dusty village road, he waved gaily and wondered with a broad grin what queer turn of circumstance brought him into the village like a conqueror, he who had been virtually imprisoned for the past week. What would Dad and Manu say now?

Chapter Eleven
Manjli's Plan

Strangely enough, on Pradhan's return neither the chief nor Manu cut the atmosphere with their threats. Salku and his younger brothers had spied the motorcycle coming down the road Sunday afternoon about four o'clock. Their eyes opened wide with admiration when they recognized their older brother riding with the missionary, and they ran along behind.

Nor could they wait until the baptismal service had transpired and Pradhan had returned home! They went to meet him at the bank of the stream, and grasping his hand, Puchu asked, "What's it feel like to ride the phut-phutia?"

Pradhan looked down and smiled. "I'll tell you when I get home, Puchu. Perhaps you'll have a chance some day."

A sulky Manu listened to the boys interrogating their new hero on his return to the courtyard. He decided this wasn't the auspicious time to needle his rival, so he discreetly left. In fact, Pradhan enjoyed several days of release from the bickering that had become the norm in Raghu's home.

But whereas the boys now clung to their older brother, Manjli and Raghu sensed Manu's crafty lurking in the shadows. Manjli became more and more apprehensive, and her opposition to her husband's attending the mission more and more pronounced. The chief encouraged her to vigilance, but the net result of her two months' struggle brought no change in Pradhan's behavior. She was sure her husband still visited the white-haired preacher every evening, despite her urgent pleas to watch his step.

Why should the chief pressure me, she thought rebelliously. Regardless of what I say or do, that Benjamin continues to mesmerize my husband.

Her thoughts paced her grinding out spices for the evening's

78

curry, and she pounded away to vent her feelings. There
. . . there . . . there . . . that's what you get, Pradhan, for
endangering my position in this village! Didn't I marry you
because you would be chief? Bang . . . swish water to moisten
the spices . . . bang them again. . . .

The young woman tossed her head defiantly and thought,
I'll leave him if he becomes a Christian. Maybe I won't even wait
that long. . . .

Once desertion entered Manjli's mind, it kept recurring. But
it posed problems that required careful planning, so the young
woman gave it much thought.

One morning she met a former friend at the village well.
"Sanjli!" she exclaimed, "what are you doing here? I haven't seen
you for years!"

The two women contrasted considerably, Manjli with her
tall, dignified bearing, her patrician features and hair combed
straight back, with bun at the neck. Sanjli had retained her baby
looks, her girlish giggle, and hair softly waving around her face,
tied back loosely with a bit of colored ribbon. She looked at the
older girl and laughed, "We're visiting my husband's uncle. He
lives in Khanua."

"Oh, I didn't know. Remember the last time we met?"

Sanjli giggled, then answered, "Sure! Ramu and I eloped
that night!"

Manjli laughed in response, then answered, "I recall. We
girls were dancing at the fair, and we suddenly realized you were
missing . . . and so was your young man."

"All planned," Sanjli replied as she rested her filled water pot
on the wall. "I kept my eye on him while he danced with the young
men. I watched him leave the line and stand under a tree to the
left. When his umbrella went up, I knew what to do."

"Did the marriage last?"

"Yes, he's my husband, and we have three children."

"Really? You still look like the little girl I knew. You've
hardly aged in the last five years."

"Good of you to say so!"

"Where are you living?"

"In a village near Murliganj, not too far from here. Come
and see us."

"Oh, I will," her friend promised. Manjli let the bucket and rope down as she talked, then drew the water up, hand over hand, and filled one vessel. Sanjli watched, then said, "My husband's uncle is ill, so we came to visit, and moreover . . ."

"Yes?" Manjli glanced at her companion, sensing her embarrassment.

"We heard there's a Christian mission here, and we'd like to see it."

"Oh?" By sheer willpower the chief's daughter-in-law restrained her anger to ask, "Are you interested in Christians?"

"Not really. I haven't had much contact with them, but a new mission is under construction south of Murliganj. I've heard that two Santals have already become Christians. They went through some strange water rite. I'd like to see it."

Manjli's countenance changed as a plan began to form in her mind. She asked, "They're building a mission, you say? Do they need laborers?"

"Yes, they do in fact. . . . A group of Santals from our village are working there, both men and women. They're carrying loads of mud and brick for the masons." She paused, then continued, "The workers have built quite a camp settlement."

Pradhan's wife filled her second water pot, then asked, "Santals? Do they earn a decent wage?"

"Oh, yes! Christians are different from other people."

"How, Sanjli?"

"They pay Santals the same as Hindus and Muslims."

"Really? Are you sure?"

Sanjli gave her friend a quick look. "Of course!" she exclaimed. "Why do you ask?"

Manjli shrugged. "I need some extra money," she explained with a smile. "We could go for a month or two since the field work is slack right now. I'll ask my husband and father-in-law. Sanjli, I'm so glad we met today! I'll come and see you when we get to Murliganj."

"Good! Then we'll take time for a proper visit. Ask any of the workers from Birpur and they'll tell you how to find us."

The young women picked up their water pots. Manjli placed one on her head and held it secure with her right hand. She stooped slightly to grasp the second pot with her left hand and carefully lifted it, holding it to her side. The girls' queenly, measured steps safely traversed the dusty road back to the village.

That evening Manjli scrutinized her husband's face. Deciding he was in a receptive mood, she ventured, "I had an interesting experience today. I met an old friend who lives near Murliganj. Sanjli says a new Christian mission is being erected south of town."

Pradhan cast his wife a quick, searching glance. Why this interest? He merely nodded and prompted her by saying, "Well?"

"She says many Santals from Birpur have found jobs there, and they're well paid. She says the Christians pay Santals as much as Hindus or Moslems. Since we don't have much fieldwork now and could use extra money, I was wondering . . . " Her voice trailed into silence.

"Wondering what?"

"Wouldn't it be a good chance for us? Your father might permit us to go if you ask him."

Pradhan scanned his wife's face. Manjli? What motivated her? Was she secretly considering the Christian message? His heart leaped in hope.

The chief consented to his son's request since he felt Manjli would surely prevent her husband from becoming more involved with Christians. Moreover, leaving home might break Benjamin's hold over him.

Pradhan and his family traveled by train to Murliganj. Then they walked the mile to the new mission site and asked a mason, "Could we get a job?"

"There's the foreman," he answered, indicating a man under a mango tree. "His name is Paul Soren."

Paul agreed and suggested they report for work the next morning. Now the family tackled the job of housing. In the mango grove, fifty yards from the construction site, they erected a small grass-thatch hut as others had done. It was in a good location and part of the little Santal village. Now Manjli found the older girl who cared for small children and arranged the care of her two little ones during work hours.

For a week Pradhan's wife carried bricks while her husband aided the masons. She had safely completed phase one, and she figured phase two of her plan should be equally simple.

Life settled into a routine of work for the parents, and joy for the children. Four-year-old Jatha shouted with glee as he joined others wallowing happily on the wet bricks that the workers kept dousing with water. Even the chief's grandson clapped his hands and gurgled with joy.

In the evenings, at the close of each work day, Santal men walked to the bazaar to buy food while their women busied themselves at their homemade stoves stoked with leaves and twigs for fuel. The fragrance of rice and curried lentils soon filled the evening air while the men sat in a circle and swapped stories during the long twilight. A common sense of community strengthened them for life among the *dikkus*. Just before time to retire each man would rejoin his family for his one main meal a day.

A week after their arrival in this shack settlement, Pradhan returned from market to find the hut empty. He called, "Manjli, Manjli," but heard no answer. He went to the pump, then back to the hut. A closer scrutiny in the shack caused a shock. Both Manjli's and the children's clothes were missing! Her week's money had gone, too!

His mind whirled. An emergency at home? Had his father called for her return? If so, why didn't she tell him? Perhaps Manjli left a message. He questioned the girl who cared for the children.

"Did Jatha's mother say where she was going?"

"No, sir. Just said she wanted the baby, and picked him up."

He turned away disheartened, went back to the hut and quickly made a cup of tea and ate some mangoes. Then he sought the foreman.

"Paul," he said, "please may we go home for several days? There's trouble, apparently, and my wife has already left."

"Why, yes, Pradhan. Do you expect to return?"

"I think so. I just want to check things out."

"Then I'll hold your place. You're a good worker."

The chief's son cast him a grateful glance. He needed that word of encouragement right now. He stuffed several mangoes into his shoulder bag, picked up his few belongings and hit the trail. In this bright moonlight he could make faster time by trekking cross-country, rather than waiting for the night train to

Banmankhi, then changing for Barhara Kothi. A sense of urgency prodded him.

As he walked in the stillness of the night, his restlessness lessened. He remembered his former walk with Benjamin, and he could hear the converted witch doctor say, "It costs, Pradhan. The price of following Jesus is high, but he's worth it."

The young man prayed aloud, "I can pay the price if you're with me, Lord." Suddenly he knew he wasn't alone. The Presence walked with him, refreshing his heart and mind with the memories of that other memorable day that ended in their first pact together. He relived his first meeting with God out under the stars—the pain and fear, followed by the vision of a risen Lord. He heard the words, "I came to deliver you . . . you don't need to struggle alone . . . I conquered Satan . . . you can conquer through me. . . ."

He remembered his commitment—the same words he had just reiterated, "If you're with me, Lord." He recalled sitting up in bed and saying aloud, "I give myself to you now. I'm yours, and you are my Lord."

These intervening months had strengthened that bond. He lifted his face to the heavens as he stopped under a tree to rest and said, "Thank you, thank you, Jesus!"

A quiet sense of direction encompassed him. Pradhan now knew he must meet Benjamin, not his father.

About three-thirty next morning the chief's son reached the mission site and stood by Benjamin's bed in the schoolhouse courtyard. "Benjamin . . . Pastor Benjamin," he called softly, touching the sleeping form.

The preacher arose, rubbed his eyes, then motioned the guest to sit beside him. "What is it, son?" he asked. "Is there trouble?"

"That's what I'm wondering. Is something wrong at home?"

"Not that I've heard. You didn't stay long in Murliganj. What brings you here?"

"My wife and children have gone." Pradhan's shoulders drooped.

"Is it now?" Benjamin answered in amazement. "Why?"

"I don't know, Pastor. We didn't quarrel. Since the Lord changed me, I don't lose my temper like I used to."

"But what about Manjli? Has she changed? You said she's been spying on your movements through your cousin Manu, under your father's instigation. Has Manjli changed?"

"I don't know. She asked to go to Murliganj, and I hoped it meant a change of heart."

"It could," the older man said thoughtfully, pulling the sheet around his shoulders to keep off the chill. "Yes, it might mean she's not happy to fight you longer, but doesn't know how to get out of her commitments."

"Or it could be the opposite," the young man said miserably.

"What do you mean?"

"She talked of leaving me if I'd become a Christian," he replied, "but that was quite awhile ago. I don't know how she feels now."

Benjamin rubbed his forehead thoughtfully and blinked several times. "You'd better stay away from home, Pradhan," he said. "If your father hears your wife and children have left, he may think you have hurt them. It would give him and Manu good reason to kill you. They've threatened, haven't they?"

"Yes, Pastor, but I've never regarded my father's threat seriously. I believe he really loves me, although he's not a person to show any sign of affection. I don't want to hurt him, and that's the reason I've held back from baptism this long."

Benjamin wiped his eyes with the corner of his sheet, then answered, "I know. Pradhan, we must work carefully now, and not spoil God's plan. Where do you think Manjli has gone?"

The young man looked blank, then straightened and said, "I'd guess she's gone to her parents. If she's walked out on me, she'd go home. I'm sure she would."

"In that case, you'd better go after her. The chief need never know you've been here. Go, son, quietly . . . before the village awakes. Meet me tomorrow noon at Orrahi railway station when the Banmankhi train comes in."

"Please pray for me first, Pastor. You know what a terrible temper I have."

"But you're not the old Pradhan, you know. Jesus Christ will hold you. You do belong to him, don't you?" The white-haired pastor nodded and smiled, then continued, "He'll walk with you and see you through everything. Now, let's pray."

Pradhan left with new peace. He strode rapidly, aware of the first streaks of dawn beginning to lighten the eastern sky. And, as Benjamin had promised, the Presence walked with him.

Thank you, Jesus, his heart sang. He looked at God's beautiful creation with new eyes. The doves cooed in the early morning freshness. Sparrows twittered, and across the fields came the occasional cry of the peacock punctuating the monotonous call of the brainfever bird.

The sun peeped over the horizon, and overhead fleecy white clouds floated lazily by. Soon the tepid heat would force him to rest under the shade of a tree for several hours. What a blissful thought! Ah! Then he would sleep . . . but now, let him cover the miles.

A gnawing hunger pain reminded Pradhan he hadn't eaten much last evening. At the next bazaar he bought some Indian bread and curried potatoes. A refreshing cup of hot tea finished his meal. He again took to the trail, walking southwest. Manjli's journey from Murliganj the day before was considerably shorter, he reflected. She must have reached home by early nightfall.

The sun hung low in the heavens as the weary traveler entered the Santal village where Manjli's parents lived. He strode now with confidence, sure she would never divulge his interest in Christianity. He could almost hear her say, "Pradhan's working on a building project in Murliganj, so I've come to visit for several weeks. I knew you wanted to see your grandchildren."

"Yes, Manjli would say that," he muttered as he turned into their courtyard.

The young woman looked up from the mat where she was gathering grain. She straightened in amazement, bracing herself for the blow the old Pradhan would have given. A thought raced through her mind—it's good Jatha's at the neighbors and my parents have gone to market! Let's get this over with!

But instead of striking her, Pradhan walked over to the verandah. Had her husband hit her, she could have borne it. She watched him pick up his younger son. He smiled as he fondled the lad and faced his wife. "Tell me about it, Manjli," he said. "Why did you come?"

She stepped back, then sat weakly on the edge of the verandah. This new behavior completely baffled her. She cried out, "Are you going to become a Christian?"

"Yes, of course."

"Then I'm not going to live with you!" She spat in his face.

Pradhan winced. Her violent reaction shocked him. He saw her face now distorted with anger. Manjli stood up, grabbed the baby, and holding the lad close, hissed at her husband, "Traitor! You aren't a Santal! You . . . you . . . you are a . . . witch!"

Her husband instinctively raised his arm to strike, but instead it fell and he drew a deep breath. In that moment the woman dashed into the house. Clasping her baby, she stood inside the door and snapped, "Now I'm in my own home. You have no further control over me. When you return to your senses, I'll talk. Not until then!" She spit again, then slammed the door. Its thud reverberated into the depths of Pradhan's soul.

He turned slowly and left the courtyard. Her derision pierced as a sharp knife, a pain he'd never experienced. "She's the mother of my children, and I love her," he whispered to the One who kept step with him. "Please, Jesus, help me."

As he walked the village trail toward Orrahi a cool breeze touched his flushed face. It came from heaven, a sweet whisper that he wasn't alone, and in the strength of that comfort the man faced his personal Gethsemane. Even though numbed by pain, Pradhan felt grace flowing over him, sustaining and strengthening him in his tragic hour.

That night he slept fitfully on a bench at Orrahi's station platform. He heard the Lord say, "I've experienced rejection, too. . . . Just trust me." And he bowed again and said, "Yes, Lord."

Tomorrow Pradhan would meet Benjamin.

Chapter Twelve

Intervention

Pradhan pulled his cotton sheet around his head and shoulders to protect himself from the morning chill. Nearby, travelers lined up at the raspy hand-pump for a quick wash before the train arrived from Banmankhi in the early morning. A vendor's monotone calling out "*Chai garam, chai garam*" (hot tea) reminded the chief's son that breakfast would be most welcome. But he could afford to wait until the train had come and gone. With a half day on his hands, he idly watched the flurry of activity at the railway station. When it simmered down, he walked the dusty road to the bazaar to buy a hearty breakfast.

About noon, back at the station, Pradhan spotted a familiar figure walking the trail from Jhungi. The young man's heart lightened as he strode forward to meet the preacher.

"Son, we're going to Banmankhi," Benjamin volunteered. "You didn't know?" he added, noting Pradhan's surprise. "Run and buy two tickets quickly."

Pradhan sprinted to the station and joined the line at the ticket window. Five minutes later, tickets in hand, they watched the train round the bend. It puffed, snorted, and blew billows of black smoke. When it came to a screeching halt, passengers rushed to the nearest open door. But Benjamin and Pradhan walked to the front of the train where they found an almost empty compartment. "Let's sit here," the preacher said. "We can talk without interference. Now tell me what happened."

They spoke softly in Santali, as the several passengers at the other end carried on their own animated conversation. As Pradhan talked, the older man occasionally interrupted with a question, but for the most part, he listened. Finally he said, "You can't

87

force Manjli, Pradhan. She has chosen, and God and the community respect choices."

"But how can I win her back without renouncing my faith?" he cried. "Pastor, she's my wife!"

"I know, but she's also an adult, like you. You have chosen to follow Jesus; she has decided against him. You'll have to wait and let the Lord work this out. But we'll do what we can to help. Remember, my son, we aren't left without a powerful weapon in our hands."

"What's that?" the distressed man asked.

Benjamin looked out the window at the passing scenery. His eyes gleamed as he turned to his companion and answered, "Prayer! I'm trusting the Lord to reveal himself to Manjli and bring her back to you—as a believer!"

The young man drew a deep breath. "Isn't that too much? He could hear her say, "You . . . you . . . you're a . . . witch!"

"Never too much," the older man declared softly. "Not if you trust the Lord Jesus implicitly."

"I've promised to trust him, and I know he's faithful, but I wish I could trust myself. . . . "

Pastor Benjamin smiled, "How human we are! Yes, you're right, my son. We can fully trust the Lord to keep his word, but we wonder at our own fickleness, don't we? But there again, turn yourself over to him, and let him keep you."

"I wish I could. . . . "

"You can, if you will. Will you?"

Pradhan nodded numbly.

"You're not alone. The Lord is with you." Pradhan heard the words as a benediction and murmured, "I know, but I find the wound so fresh, it's hard to trust, even though I want to."

The older man laid his hand on the younger man's knee and said softly, "I believe God is going to bring your wife back to you."

"How can you be so sure?" The young man heard the clicking of the wheels on the rails. They seemed to sing monotonously, "She's gone from you . . . she's gone from you . . . she's gone from you."

He turned to his companion and said hopelessly, "She's

gone from me! Your family is also separated. Your wife and son live in Santal Parganas while you and Dina live here."

Benjamin chuckled, then responded, "You're right, and I accept that until my wife and I are one in spirit. But that doesn't mean God is finished with us yet. The timing and details remain in his hands."

"Then how can you be so cheerful?"

"Simply because I've turned it over to him, so it's his business, not mine! He tells us to do this, Pradhan. You must cast your burden on the Lord, and he will sustain you. See here?" Benjamin opened his Bible and the two bent over the Scriptures.

That heart-to-heart talk resulted in a new perspective for Pradhan. Benjamin eased the pain by accompanying him to Murliganj and stayed with him several days while visiting Dharkola and other nearby villages. The preacher and chief's son spent long evening hours studying the Word until the young man learned to rejoice in suffering for Christ's sake.

Benjamin's time in the camp proved beneficial in bringing several other Santals into Paul Soren's home for prayer and fellowship, and the group began praying fervently for Manjli's restoration to her husband.

A month later Pradhan returned home with money for the family. His father was visibly pleased.

"But where are your wife and sons?" he asked.

"With her parents. She's visiting them for awhile."

That ended the matter, except for the Christians' daily intercession. They pleaded, "Bring Manjli back, dear Lord. Reveal yourself to her and bring her back—soon!"

In her parents' home, thirty miles southwest of Khanua, Manjli's fury spent itself after the first ten days and gave way to memory. She relived sitting under the stars, hearing again the Christian stories and sweet lyrics about Jesus and his love. She felt the tug at her heart, the desire to know this one about whom the Christians sang, and in retrospect she now wondered where they found their joy and peace. Dina, Miriam, and Martha—they seemed so content, so sure!

But the girl vacillated between intense desire and a sense of guilt and fear. The evil spirits would surely curse her and her children for Pradhan's interest in another religion. Her parents must never suspect his waywardness, nor her former interest. If they learned her true reason for coming home, they'd cast her out immediately, lest evil spread its menacing tentacles over them also.

Manjli filled her days with work, but she dreaded the nights. On her mat, with the baby held close, and her son Jatha sleeping nearby, the young woman tossed from side to side. Night after night she puzzled over the question, is it true? Is Jesus greater than *Marang Buru*? Did he really conquer Satan, and if so, as the Christians claim, is that victory still valid today?

Seven, eight, nine weeks passed. One night, after hours of searching and longing for peace, Manjli cried out, "Jesus, if you're real, please tell me. If I could be sure, I'd give myself to you. I want peace."

She fell asleep and dreamed.

In her dream Manjli saw herself seated on the verandah, a Bible open in her lap. She was pointing out words and reading slowly, "In my Father's house are many mansions: if it were not so, I would have told you. I go to prepare a place for you. . . . "

Joy and peace surged within as she mouthed the Lord's promises again and again. But underneath the joy a deep sorrow made it a bitter-sweet experience. Manjli, Pradhan's widow, had held her husband back from believing!

Where was he now? Certainly not with Jesus. . . .

His burial rites had just been concluded as drums beat and men drank rice beer to drown their intense grief. More drinking, more carousing to erase the memory of the tragic death of the chief's son, accidentally gored by a wounded boar.

Manjli cried aloud in her dream, "He'd be with Jesus if I hadn't opposed him! He wanted to believe, but I called him a traitor, a witch! Oh, God, forgive! Please allow me another chance. Please, Lord Jesus!"

The intensity of that cry awakened her. The woman looked around. Jatha and the baby slept serenely. Manjli shook herself, then began to laugh, and said aloud, "It's a dream! It's a dream! It's not true!"

Not true? She stopped, wondering whether it just might be true—that Pradhan had been accidentally killed, that he had drawn back from following Jesus. She must find out! She must!

"Lord Jesus, oh, Lord Jesus," she panted, "please let it be only a dream! I'm sorry I held him back, and I promise I'll never do it again. Now I know you're true. You sent me that dream. Please, Lord Jesus, give me a second chance."

The household began to stir in the early dawn. Manjli dressed quickly, gathered her possessions, then awakened her children. After preparing a lunch for the journey, she bade her parents farewell.

"We've had a good visit," she said, "but I must return now to my husband. He needs me."

"Yes, daughter, go," they agreed.

Manjli lifted her bundle on her head. She took Jatha by the hand, and placed the baby on her hip. Walking tall and straight, she returned to find her husband to ask his forgiveness.

Because of the length of the journey, Manjli decided to head for Murliganj and catch the train there for Banmankhi and then Barhara Kothi. It was a round-about way but it would save much weariness on the part of the children.

By ten in the morning the woman reached the construction site and inquired as to Pradhan's whereabouts. "He hasn't worked here for the last several weeks," Paul Soren replied. "He said his father needed him in the fields." Paul looked at the woman and asked, "Where have you come from now?"

"My parents," she answered, then continued with an embarrassed grin, "Mr. Paul, I ran away with the children because I determined to leave Pradhan if he becomes a Christian."

"Yes?" he said with a smile, "and what brings you back?"

"A dream . . . " she began, then blurted out, "Please, Mr. Paul, tell me, is my husband still following Jesus? Is he all right?"

"As far as I know," the man answered. "Would you like to talk to my wife, Naomi? She's at home."

"Oh, could I?"

"Most certainly. Just go over and tell her I sent you. Stay with us for lunch. It will give the children a chance to sleep while you talk. I'll be home at noon, and we'll see that you catch the early afternoon train for Banmankhi. That should get you back to Khanua by evening."

"Thank you, thank you, Mr. Paul."

She turned to go, but he added, "You should know that Pradhan worked here for about a month after you left. Our little group of Christians have been praying daily for you."

"Really? I didn't know anybody cared."

"We care very much. Naomi will tell you. We've been praying for your quick return to save Pradhan from unnecessary pressure from his family."

"Oh, thank you. How can I ever thank you?"

As Manjli reviewed that amazing experience in Paul Soren's home, she knew the miracle of tears mingled with joy, the strengthening bond of Christian fellowship and prayer support. Throughout her train journey she relived those two wonderful hours, and her heart leaped in anticipation. If meeting fellow believers is like this, what will it mean to have a husband who prays and shares with me, she wondered. Even as she nursed the baby and kept Jatha happy, her own beautiful face radiated a joy that caused other passengers to notice her.

It was getting dark by the time she reached Khanua. A quick glance took in the empty courtyard. Manjli opened the door to their house and peered inside. All was dark in the gathering twilight of a warm summer evening. Laying the sleeping baby and her bundle on the bed, the young woman lit a lantern. She looked around and smiled. Pradhan had kept the house neat and clean.

She hummed softly as one of the Christian lyrics they had learned in those outdoor meetings came back to her, and Manjli's countenance glowed with inner joy.

Jatha barely managed the lunch his mother fed him. From sheer exhaustion he fell asleep. His mother tiptoed out, then called a boy passing on the road. "Sumi," she said, "run over to the mission and tell Pradhan we've come. Please! Hurray!"

Five minutes later the door burst open and Pradhan rushed in. One look at Manjli's transformed countenance told the story. He took her in his arms and whispered, "Manjli! You've come! And you're more beautiful than I've ever seen you. . . . "

Tears welled up and overflowed as she hid her face on his shoulder. She pleaded, "Forgive me! Oh, forgive me for calling you a traitor and a witch. I didn't understand. Please forgive me."

He held her close. "My love, I forgave you long ago," he murmured. "Do you want to tell me about it?"

"But I must know something else first," she said urgently, looking into his face. "Pradhan, do you love Jesus?"

"Of course," he answered, baffled. "Did you think I didn't?"

"I wanted to be sure," she whispered. "Come, let's sit on the verandah so we don't waken the boys."

Her story tumbled out as they sat together on the steps. In the light of the flickering lantern set nearby, the young man was entranced with the glow on his wife's face. She told of her frustrations, her emptiness and fears, her sense of guilt, and her longings to know whether Jesus is real. Then she shared the startling dream, so pivotal that it had transformed her life.

"The Lord gave you that dream, Manjli," Pradhan said softly. "We've been praying for you."

"I know. Paul and Naomi told me. And now I won't hold you back ever, anymore. . . . "

"Do you believe, my love?"

"Yes," she said in a whisper. "I've given myself to Jesus, too."

"Will you take baptism with me?"

"Give me a little time," she answered. "Let me learn a little more."

"It is good," he said. "We'll wait together, and learn the meaning of true Christian marriage. When the time comes, dearest, both of us will be ready."

She nodded, the glow of anticipation on her beautiful face, and the Presence hovered near and enfolded them both.

Chapter Thirteen
Dulu's Decisions

"So you've come!" Pradhan's mother snapped the next morning. She scrutinized her daughter-in-law and noted a new beauty. The older woman grimaced, then grumbled, "I must say you took your time . . . even though you must have known we're overworked."

Manjli drew a deep breath, but answered softly, "Sorry, Ma. Field work is further advanced here than at my home. It's just starting. See? I've brought you some rice and bananas."

"Hmmm . . . " the older woman grunted as she took the gift.

Not even a word of thanks? Manjli straightened, reminding herself she could expect nothing but conflict. Hadn't she lived with it the past five years? With wedding negotiations beginning for Salku, second eldest, perhaps the new bride would prove more compatible with the family. Pradhan's wife sincerely hoped so.

But despite her difficulties that first day, she knew an inner joy, as though some little bird trilled inside, "I belong to Jesus! He's with me, and I needn't fear anymore."

Moreover, the girl looked at her mother-in-law with new understanding. Why hadn't she noticed those gnarled hands and drawn features? And that bent back? This woman had lived a hard life. She knew the heartache of losing two children at childbirth, leaving her with four boys to rear. She lived with a man who seemed devoid of affection, cold and austere. As his wife, it was her place to maintain his welfare and status, and to lead the women of the village. Manjli now looked at her mother-in-law and wondered, is it possible she was also beautiful when

94

young? Could it be she's bitter now because of having lost her youth?

With compassion welling up, Manjli acknowledged, "Ma, my absence did make it harder for you. I should have come earlier, but I didn't realize."

The older woman looked directly into the girl's face and said, "What's happened to you? You're different!"

Manjli smiled, and began spreading the grains to dry in one corner of the courtyard. The chief and his young brother, Dulu, were chatting over near the house. Raghu looked at Manjli and called, "Come here, daughter."

He stopped his rope-making as she approached and bowed low before him. He acknowledged the gesture by lifting his right hand in blessing.

"Yes, sir?" Manjli inquired, standing demurely before him.

"Daughter, your husband attended the Christian mission regularly during your absence. He's stubborn. I want you to watch him constantly and turn his mind from this crazy obsession."

Dulu, though leaning idly against a post, tensed. He watched Manjli draw a deep breath and heard her say, "Please, forgive me, sir. I've given this much thought." Dulu knew Pradhan's yearning for his wife to come to faith, and he felt his being there was more than providential. He must act in Pradhan's behalf.

The girl continued with downcast eyes, "Perhaps I have been wrong when I opposed him. Could there be truth in the Christian message? Please permit me to search for myself. I seek release from my promise to deter my husband so that I may honestly face this matter."

"What?" the chief shouted. His face flushed with anger, and he leaped to his feet to strike, but Dulu caught his arm and said, "You don't hit her!"

Raghu spun in fury. "You, too?" he demanded.

"Yes, sir! My brother, you have held us back long enough. All we ask is a chance to search honestly. I understand what she's saying. It's a fair request."

The chief collapsed on his mat. Dulu continued, "I want you to listen to me. Look, you desire the best for your people. I know you do. Raghu, lead us into the worship of the true God. Stop objecting when we seek release from the oppression of the *bongas*."

"Hold your tongue, you fool!"

"Fool or no, I have something to say. I request the right to speak."

"Then speak!"

"Can we lightly bypass the testimony of a man who served the evil spirits for years? One who led witch doctors in a large area of our homeland?"

"Bah! He's a fake," the chief growled, and stood to his feet.

"How do you know?" his brother challenged. "Have you tested him? Have you ever asked him to play the rhythms for you? If he's counterfeit, he won't know them. If he's genuine, he will. It's as simple as that."

Manjli quietly watched the two men, so alike in build, yet representing two different generations. Pradhan had told her Dulu came along years later, born to his grandfather's second wife after Raghu had already married and was well established. Now Pradhan's father looked at his young brother and prompted, "Well? Do you want to follow this foreign religion, Dulu?"

The young man faced him quietly and said, "I'm seriously considering it. But I wish we could believe as a family, to save dissension." He stepped back and looked the chief fully in the face, then added, "But if you and Guru continue to oppose, I'm giving you warning, sir, I'm not going to wait."

"Fool!" Raghu hissed. He picked up his tobacco pouch, took a pinch and began rolling a cigarette. Dulu answered, "Raghu, consider me a fool if you like, but I remind you that half of your people share my sentiments. We seek freedom to investigate for ourselves."

The chief regarded him craftily. "Oh?" he inquired. "So you object to my rule?"

Dulu shook his head. "No, sir," he replied, "I've been loyal to you from the first. Even now, I'm sure you oppose our becoming Christians because you haven't made investigation for yourself. Please . . . " the man pleaded, "lead us in our search, Raghu. Lead us to the knowledge and worship of Thakur Jiu."

Coldness settled over the chief's features. He turned to

Manjli and said, "You have your request. Search! But you now cut yourself off from our family. As Pradhan's wife and mother of his children, you may live with him. But neither you, nor he, will eat again with us, nor will you have any part in family matters."

She bowed low, then returned to her work.

That evening Manjli recounted the incident to Pradhan in the privacy of their own quarters. "Manjli!" He seized her and swung her around. "I'm proud of you!"

A bit breathless, she giggled, then said, "We've just lost one big worry, Pradhan."

"What's that?"

"Their poisoning our food!" She exploded into laughter, then continued more seriously as she began to straighten her clothes and hair. "One of these days your uncle is going to request baptism. He really fought for me and for all of us who are interested in Christianity. He surprised me, Pradhan. He's usually very quiet."

Her husband drew a deep breath, then said, "But this means my dad will now turn to Manu. You've helped keep his heart open to me in the past, Manjli."

"Perhaps so, although both of us were terribly mean to you." She turned to face her husband. Placing her hands on his shoulders, she looked deep into his eyes and said, "We have Jesus, Pradhan. And for the first time this Sunday we can attend the service together and take our children. Does that help to make up for your father's disfavor?"

The pain in his eyes slowly gave way to a gleam of joy and he said, "Forgive me, my love, for thinking of myself instead of you and the boys." He took her in his arms, then continued, "What is the loss of my father when it means the acquiring of my family? Dear God, I'm blessed! Look at my beautiful wife, and my two sons."

"They'll have the chance now to become godly men," Manjli added softly. "We don't have a divided house any longer."

Sunday worship services in the schoolhouse always showed

good attendance. Benjamin's violin and homespun messages became the leading event in Khanua's otherwise drab existence. Among the broad spectrum of attendees, a few came to spy, some to worship, but for the greater part, Benjamin's audience welcomed release from boredom.

Therefore a general rustle of interest followed the preacher's announcement, "The Banmankhi Sahib and Memsahib will visit us this weekend, and we'll plan special meetings. All who desire baptism, please see me."

Pradhan's pulsebeat quickened. Would he? Could he? His father decided for him.

On Saturday morning the chief called his eldest son. "I'm sending you to a village near Katihar, Pradhan," he said. "It's an urgent message. Here." Raghu handed him a sealed envelope. The young man bowed, pushing back his thoughts. He didn't see his father's eyes narrow as the chief recalled his urgent message: "Keep him until Sunday afternoon."

Before taking the trail, however, Pradhan slipped next door. "Dulu," he said disconsolately, "my father is sending me on what he terms an urgent mission. Please tell Benjamin Pastor and the others I really wanted to be with them."

Dulu put his hand on his shoulder and said, "Buddy, it's all right. Don't worry. When God's time comes for you to step out, nobody will hinder." A look of understanding passed between the two, and with squared shoulders, the chief's son turned and left for Orrahi, six miles distant, where he would get the train.

Dulu watched him go. Guru hides behind excuses, he mused, and Pradhan fights family interference. Why am I waiting? I have neither . . . since I own my own house and land.

During the Sunday morning service six Santals applied for baptism, including Patras's wife and another couple from a nearby village. All applicants had publicly witnessed to their faith in Jesus Christ. A hush settled over the audience as the pastor asked quietly, "Is anyone else ready to follow the Lord in baptism today?"

Heads turned and a ripple of astonishment swept through the congregation as the young brother of the chief stood. "Yes, Dulu?" Benjamin inquired. "Do you desire to speak?"

"Thank you, Pastor," he said clearly. "From the time we had

meetings in this village, I have left the worship of the *bongas*. I believe in Jesus, and I love him. Moreover, I know he loves me. I have heard his call to follow, and I request baptism today."

Benjamin couldn't contain his joy. "Praise God!" he exclaimed. "Amen!"

Manjli, sitting with her children on either side, thought—one of these days it will be our turn. I hope it's soon.

The baptismal service prefaced a delicious feast prepared by the ladies of the group. After all had eaten, the believers then formed a circle and prayed fervently for courage to stand in the face of persecution. They sang a parting song, went through the ceremonial bowing and giving of blessings, then turned homeward. Where no church had been, now a functioning body manifested itself.

Gopal Singh heard the news and vowed revenge. "Become a Christian," he muttered, "and you lose your land."

Some of the villagers cringed in fear, among them Daniel's father. "See what you've done to us?" he cried. "You Christians have angered the *bongas*, and taken away our livelihood."

Benjamin spoke up fearlessly, "The Lord will deal with the 'lion.' Remember, our God has the last word."

One family, however, did not upset Gopal Singh. On the outskirts of Khanua four brothers shared a hut. The parents had died, leaving the brothers to fend for themselves. Two were lepers who stayed home and nursed their illness. Yet all four attended the village meetings, sitting discreetly off to one side. Now the second eldest brother began to frequent the Sunday services at the mission.

Though crippled by a spinal malformity, Phagu was known to be a good worker, responsible, and of excellent spirit. He cared for his brothers, kept their vessels clean, and sought to make their days pleasant. His friends often gave Phagu odd jobs and shared their produce with him. Somehow, the brothers managed to live.

Phagu's intelligence and character matched his magnificent physique, from waist up! His smile lit his handsome features, topped by a heavy head of hair. He soon became a trusted member of the inner circle around Benjamin.

One day Phagu brought a request from his family. "Benjamin, Pastor," he said, "we believe in Jesus. We want to be baptized."

That baptismal service took place in the stream near the village during the time Pradhan was working in Murliganj. The two sick brothers had to be placed carefully into the water, but both gave clear witness to faith in Jesus Christ and went through the rite joyfully. Their teenaged brother came next, to be followed last of all by Phagu. His name became Philip.

When Gopal Singh heard the news he shrugged it off by saying, "Lepers! They want handouts from the Christians! Bah! What sort of religion is this?"

Yet Philip Murmu and his brothers now knew an acceptance never before experienced. Dressed in clean shirts and *dhotis*, Philip and his young brother Timothy attended every service.

But tragedy struck not long after that memorable baptismal service. The two sick brothers contracted an epidemic virus and died within days of each other. Soon young Timothy began to show a swelling around his ear lobes, and was sent off to the leprosarium in Bhagalpur for early treatment.

Philip was now alone.

One day he approached Pastor Benjamin and said, "Please, Pastor, would you mind if I married Martha? I would like to establish a Christian home."

Benjamin blinked rapidly, then began to chuckle. "What a beautiful idea, Philip!" he exclaimed. "She was beaten and chased out as a supposed witch, you know. You don't mind?"

He lifted his head and smiled, his eyes lighting with anticipation. "I, too, come from a wretched background," he said. "You know! But I don't have leprosy. Would Martha be willing to have me?"

"Let's pray about it, and talk it over with the Banmankhi Sahib and Memsahib, son."

Several days later, on a routine visit to Banmankhi, the white-haired preacher broached the subject to the missionary.

"But what do we do about Martha's former marriage?" Allen asked with a twinkle. He had already learned to distrust his western thinking and to rely heavily on Santals for dealing with their own people and problems.

The converted witch doctor crossed his knees, blinked several times, and chuckled. Having gone through this routine, he gazed across the fields in front of the Banmankhi mission house and said, "You see, Sahib Ji, there's much to consider in 'B.C.'— unless we begin a totally new life when we come to Jesus."

"What do you mean, 'B.C.'?"

"Before Christ . . . . We come with mixed up marriages, separations, children, immorality, beatings, and drunkenness . . . to name a few, Sahib Ji. Do you know what God does with it?"

"Yes, of course, Benjamin. He puts it under the blood of his beloved Son."

"Then couldn't we do the same?"

"I suppose so. . . . You mean, nothing before accepting Jesus counts?"

"Not when my Lord has died for it and cleansed us," the pastor said with a wise nodding of his head. His eyes twinkled as he added, "That's my way of looking at it, Sahib Ji. Begin a new life with Jesus, and then live for him, regardless of what happened in the past. That's why we take new names."

"Hmmm. . . . Benjamin, that does make sense. So Philip marries Martha, if she is willing?"

"I'd say so, and I'll ask her, if you wish."

In anticipation, Philip's friends helped him tear down the old house and build a much better one near the mission. The bride and groom, so beautifully redeemed, became respected members of the community.

But other changes weren't quite so comforting. In the months prior to the Christmas retreat, a change took place in Raghu's home, one that gave his son cause for great distress.

The chief began to listen again to Manu, his nephew. Pradhan's rival had also cultivated Salku and the other boys during their elder brother's absence in Murliganj. When Pradhan returned he found the boys aligned against him, on the mere suggestion that this is where they would find the action! In search of excitement, they listened to Manu's carefully worded suggestions that they help persecute Pradhan when he took baptism. The offer appealed to them, and they became Manu's faithful helpers.

Then came the Christmas retreat.

Chapter Fourteen

What Power is This?

To Raghu, Sundays flashed danger signals, especially when the Sahib and Memsahib came from Banmankhi. The chief had noted that baptisms take place on Sundays. Day by day his apprehension grew as he watched Pradhan become more involved with the people at the mission. It seemed incredible to think his son would throw away his Santal heritage to embrace a foreign religion!

Then came the three-day Christmas retreat that began on Sunday, and concluded on Tuesday, Christmas.

This Christian festival held no meaning to Raghu. He had never heard of it, nor seen anyone observe it. Therefore, all he knew was little enough—the Christians were gathering for some reason or other, and his son, Pradhan, would likely be among them. It presented danger.

So, on Saturday evening the chief said again, "Pradhan, you dare not become a Christian! You're in line for my position, and you must never go through that water rite. Do like Guru. He's sensible. He attends the meetings, and so may you—but nothing else. If you go beyond that, we'll bind you with ropes!" Pradhan's brothers snickered and seconded their father's suggestion.

But Sunday passed without any intimation of a baptismal service, so Raghu's vigilance relaxed. The boys attended the Sunday meetings and gave enthusiastic reports.

"Dad," they said, "a guest has come from America!"

"You mean England?"

"No, Dad," Salku reiterated, "from America. We like his talks. The pastor says it in Santali after the Sahib from Madhipura says it first in Hindi, so we get it twice."

"No water rite?"

102

"No, Dad, not even a mention of it. . . . "

"That's good."

"And the music! It's great!"

"Why? Something special?"

"The foreign lady brought her instrument, and played with the pastor."

"Pastor? Who's that?"

"The converted witch doctor, Dad. That's what they call him."

"Hmmm . . . so they have their own vocabulary."

Puchu spoke up, "And they sit in straight lines on the floor, not in circles like we're used to doing."

Sitting through anything taxed Puchu's resources, Raghu thought with the hint of a smile. "You seemed to enjoy it, boys."

"Sure, Dad, it's great."

"That's the problem . . . music and light . . . so the unsuspecting get tangled quickly in their lies."

"No, Dad, we enjoy seeing what's happening. You don't need to worry about us."

"You've seen enough for this week. No more going to the mission. Hear me?"

So Pradhan's brothers weren't there on Tuesday to witness the Christians' observance of Christmas.

Early that morning Pradhan and Manjli knew this would be "his day." Before Jatha and the baby ever awakened, the parents prayed for courage and Pradhan promised, "Lord, I'll do it, by your grace." Manjli's fervent "yes" bonded husband and wife together in their resolution to obey Christ's call at any cost.

But before they left their room, Pradhan took her in his arms, looked deep into her eyes and asked, "Are you sure? It may mean my death."

"I'm sure, Pradhan," she whispered, tears glistening on her cheeks. "Our Lord will watch over both you and us."

He held her close, then said, "Come, each of us will carry a boy over to the mission. Let's get out of here before anyone suspects we're gone."

Miriam's open door policy since Martha's marriage to Philip had often drawn them, and they knew they could shelter there now. They waited in her home until time for service, then casually joined the other worshipers.

After several hours of sharing, witnessing and rejoicing, the visiting missionary, Charles Engle, asked, "Does anyone desire baptism today?"

Pradhan stood to his feet. A paean of praise arose, then simmered as the young man began to speak. "I have waited a long time," he said simply. "Now I know my waiting period is over and I request baptism today regardless of consequences."

A hush settled over the audience. All knew the chief's harsh attitude toward his son. In midafternoon, however, the Christians walked through the village to the stream. Pradhan and Manjli glanced into the chief's courtyard as they passed, but failed to see Raghu speaking to Guru and Manu. Raghu had just returned from Barhara Kothi and knew nothing of his son's testimony in the morning service. Guru and his son had spent the day in their fields, and were now returning.

The chief looked up when he heard the singing and asked casually, "Christians? What are they doing?"

"I'll find out," Manu offered. After a moment he rushed in to report, "Pradhan is to be baptized, sir . . . your son!"

"What?" the chief shrieked. "He'll die for this!"

He dashed onto the road with Guru and Manu following, but the band of Christians had already passed. Their words wafted back as they sang in Santali, "I have decided to follow Jesus. . . . No turning back, no turning back."

Livid with rage, the chief collapsed on the ground outside his home and lay there throughout the entire baptismal rite. All Guru and his son could do was to watch helplessly, and wave the flies from Raghu's face. But Puchu, happening along at that moment, took in the situation and raced down to the stream. He yelled, "My Dad has fallen! Dad has fallen!"

"What happened?" someone asked.

"He's on the road outside our house, and Uncle Guru and Manu are watching him."

"Oh!" the crowd murmured. The message came through clearly and without mistake—"Jesus felled the chief to prevent him from harming Pradhan. Jesus is greater than Satan."

A triumphant note suddenly crept into the singing. Nor did

the Christians waver when they passed the stricken man on their homeward route. In fact, they sang more lustily than before, "I have decided to follow Jesus; I'll not turn back; I'll not turn back!"

> *"Nit akawaniń Jisuiń panjaye;*
> *Bań pacok'a; bań pacok'a."*

What the chief saw or felt during that interim, nobody knows. Not until the last person had passed did he stand up and quietly enter his house. For several days the man remained mute, and when he spoke, his first words were, "I am no longer your chief. You must choose another." The Christians wondered whether Raghu had faced the King of kings.

But though Pradhan's father spoke no word against him, his family took up the cause. "Get out of this compound," his mother shrilled, "You and your family don't belong to us now."

Salku led the boys and some of the villagers in a chant, "Traitor . . . traitor . . . you're not a Santal, you're a traitor!"

Even Guru, of divided opinion, remarked that his nephew had gone too far. But his son Manu remained strangely silent. With the coveted position now within his grasp, he began to have second thoughts. The sight of his uncle sitting mute, neither condoning nor condemning the furor in the courtyard, mystified Manu. Raghu was in another world. What had happened to him? For the first time, Pradhan's rival feared.

One question demanded an answer. Who had smitten the chief to the ground? And why? Would this powerful one strike him, too, if he fought the chief's son?

So Manu held his counsel, but nobody noticed, least of all his cousins who led the heckling with glee. Yet no one lifted a hand!

Pradhan stood quietly among them, his mother's curses rising above the boys' taunts. Raghu's son waited for a long enough lull for him to do what he knew he must. The family finally hushed as they sensed his intent. They watched coldly as Pradhan removed the silver stud from his ear. Laying it at Raghu's feet, he said, "My father, I will love you always. I pray that you, too, will give your love to the Lord Jesus who gave himself for you."

Not a flicker of emotion touched the chief's face. Not a

sound escaped any onlooker's lips. But turning away, Pradhan walked over to the door of his house where Manjli had watched the ordeal in silence. Tears trickled down her cheeks as she held wondering Jatha by the hand, and the baby in the other arm. Her husband bounded up the steps, and their glances of love and understanding locked. She whispered, "I'm proud of you, Pradhan. Come, let's collect our belongings. Dulu and Maya await us."

"You're sure?" he asked.

"Yes, they told me before I left the mission."

Chapter Fifteen

Cast Out—Taken In

Although Pradhan had given no intimation to anyone that Christmas would be "his day," Dulu watched his bosom friend closely. For the past ten years they had gone on hunts together, spent their evenings in common pursuits, and of late, joined the music sessions without fail. Dulu sorely missed Pradhan during the latter's time in Murliganj, and wondered at Manjli's absence on his return. Within the day Pradhan had bared his heart to his friend.

The chief's young brother, though normally reserved, bore the respect of the community. He had chosen fearlessly to separate from Guru and Raghu when they divided the land. He built his own house next door and maintained his affairs with discretion. Throughout, Dulu found he could trust his wife Maya, small in stature, but sweet in spirit and of great discernment. Her beautiful singing voice had made her a favorite with all in the village.

Dulu and Maya had one son, born around the time of Jatha's birth, and the two boys were always together. Now they had enrolled in Dina's school, so were acquiring new reading skills. They came home singing the Christian songs, but Jatha soon learned to sing in his cousin's courtyard, rather than in his own! In fact, Maya loved the Christian lyrics, and sang them with the boys.

One day, before Manjli suggested to Pradhan they go to Murliganj, Maya's son startled her with saying, "Ma, I'm not going to be Durga any more. I want to be Samuel."

"What do you mean, son? Who's Samuel, and what's wrong with Durga?"

"You know, Ma! Durga's a Hindu god, and I don't like

107

Hindu gods . . . . I want to belong to Jesus now."

"But why Samuel?" she asked, intrigued as the boys helped her prepare vegetables for the curry.

"Dina told us about Samuel today, Ma," the boy replied.

"Yes," Jatha chimed in, "he heard God call him when he was asleep, and we want God to talk to us, too."

"Well, I think Samuel's a nice name, so I'll call you Sam. Will that be all right?"

"Yes, Ma!" The boys celebrated by turning somersaults in the front yard.

Maya told her husband about it when he came in from the field, and he laughed. She concluded, "If our five-year-old can accept Jesus, why can't I?"

"You can," the man answered softly. "I thank God that you don't oppose me like Manjli does Pradhan."

Sam sorely missed Jatha during the latter's absence, and rejoiced when he returned with his mother and baby brother. Maya saw Pradhan rushing up the road and into his courtyard.

A hasty word with Sumi who had gone to call Pradhan gave her advance news of Manjli's return.

Next morning Dulu spared Manjli from the chief's heavy fists. He mentioned the matter lightly to Maya, but didn't tell her of Manjli's change of heart.

But Dulu's wife began to notice a new glow on Manjli's face. The fact that Pradhan and Manjli and boys now attended every service at the mission caused Maya to speculate a great deal, but she didn't find the opportunity to ask the girl directly concerning the change.

About a week prior to Christmas she found Dulu busy making a divider. She asked, "What are you doing, Dulu?"

"Ah, my sweet, if I told you, you'd be surprised.

"Come, you don't keep secrets from me. What is it?"

He stopped his work and smiled, then said, "I'd better let you in on this one, Maya. It's going to affect you a great deal."

"What do you mean?" Dulu's wife laughed, her tinkling tones sounding like music.

"I'm expecting the chief to throw Pradhan and Manjli and the boys out one of these days—and we'll take them in, that is, if you're willing."

"You mean . . . you mean . . . they would live with us?"

"Yes, Maya, that's what I mean . . . but not as nephew and niece. That's ridiculous. Pradhan's been my young brother for the last ten years!"

"Manjli's awfully proud, Dulu. Do you think she'd want to come here? We live on a lower level."

"Honey, she's different. Haven't you noticed? Something's happened to both of them, and I think they'll be coming over here very soon."

Dulu and Maya worked quietly, not making any changes outwardly lest the boys take word back to Dina, and it would spread to the others. The divider took shape, then was stored for easy access. The large mats which the couple used each summer to keep out the sun's glare were now restored. Dulu could easily tie them to the verandah rafters to make walls for the new room when needed. He bought extra mats for on the floor, and at Maya's instigation, a small table and stool. She even saved a pickle jar of unusual shape for a vase, to hold a welcoming bunch of marigolds!

That Christmas morning, when Pradhan gave his testimony, Dulu knew this would be the day! After the service and the common meal, the chief's young brother slipped home to put everything in place. He fastened the mats, placed the divider, table, and stool. He even brought in marigolds to cheer up the very livable room of eight by twelve feet he had created. Then he joined the Christians for the baptismal service. A nod of his head assured Maya all was ready. She whispered to Manjli at the close of the meetings, "We're looking for you, if your family throws you out."

The girl gave her a grateful glance and answered, "Maya! How can you do that? Do you have room?"

The little woman laughed, and said, "Come and see, Manjli. We'll be waiting for you."

Somehow the road home lost some of its dread for Pradhan's wife. She took Jatha in one hand and carried the baby in her free arm as she returned to find her husband facing the curses of his mother, and the taunts of the villagers led by Salku and the other two boys.

Maya, before hurrying home, took time to invite Benjamin, Dina, and Miriam to come for her best chicken curry that night. "We'll celebrate," she said, then hurried home to hear the outcry from next door.

Dulu and Maya looked at the finished product with satisfaction. Little Samuel asked, "Who's going to live here, Ma?"

"Just wait and see," the woman replied, then gave him a hug. "You'll be pleased," she murmured. He ran out to play.

The noise increased from next door, then silence. Dulu said quietly, "Maya, I think we can look for them soon. You and I . . . we don't even know what they're going through!"

"What makes the difference?" she asked.

"We own our own home and land," he said. "I'm glad I separated from the others."

"If you hadn't, and we'd been in that courtyard with the rest, you would have had to face the same thing, Dulu."

"Yes," he said, then saw the family approaching their entrance. "Honey, they're coming!" he exclaimed.

Husband and wife hurried out to meet Pradhan and Manjli, and Samuel darted out when he saw his friend. Maya took the baby while Jatha and Samuel danced off together to play. The women went ahead, but the men lingered. Dulu placed his hand on Pradhan's shoulder and said softly, "Buddy, welcome home. This is where you belong."

The chief's son lifted his head, took a deep breath, and answered, "God bless you, Dulu. You've always been there when I needed someone. What would I do without you?"

They walked over to the house slowly, and the older answered, "I'm proud of you—Steve!"

Pradhan's hand shot out, and in that warm handclasp, with joy shining through pain, Pradhan answered, "Thanks—Andy!"

Both laughed, then relaxed. "I don't suppose we'll use our Christian names when we're alone," Dulu admitted, "but it's nice to know that both of us are beginning a new life in Jesus. Incidentally, buddy, you're no longer my nephew."

"No? Then what?"

"What you've been to me all along—my younger brother! Here's your room. Will it be all right?"

Pradhan felt all choked when he took a look. "How did you

know?" he asked. "You've prepared this just for us?"

"Of course. Maya and I've had a great time doing it. We didn't know how soon we'd need it, but I got the message this morning when you gave your testimony. Didn't you notice my absence after lunch?"

Pradhan smiled, then said, "Rather! I looked for you when we started down to the stream."

"I joined when the group passed our house. I was there, buddy, rooting for you."

"Well, that's great. Now I must bring our things over, otherwise—in their present mood—they'll confiscate them!"

"I'll come with you."

With Manjli and Maya talking happily in the kitchen and the children playing outside, the two men soon effected the change of residence. The cold stares of Pradhan's family would have chilled Pradhan again, but Dulu's comforting presence strengthened him. As night fell, the chief and his family went indoors, and Dulu and Pradhan took the last load over without interference.

Silence grasped Khanua that night. In contrast to the day of Daniel's baptism, there was no beating of drums. Khanua feared, knowing the chief sat mutely in his house, stricken by a force or power they couldn't understand. Next door, however, within the warmth of Dulu's home, his enlarged family and their beloved guests shared in singing and praise. Somehow, it became a fitting conclusion for this day of Christ's victory.

"Hold the young couple steady," the Christians prayed. All knew that Pradhan and Manjli must now face an ordeal beyond anything they had yet experienced.

Chapter Sixteen
Pradhan Pays the Price

Khanua's former chief, Raghu, had lost his haughty mein. A broken man, he maintained complete silence for about four days. When he spoke, he said, "I am no longer your chief. You must choose another." Then he called for Manjli's parents. He felt their support could pressure his son to recant from Christianity. At the least, the two sets of parents could demand a village council.

Under Raghu's insistence, the elders made Manu their interim chief, a position the young man had sought for many years. Now it had somehow lost its glamor.

The midwinter rains had set in when Manjli's parents arrived. On a cold January day Raghu and Manjli's father made their plans. It began with Raghu announcing brokenly on their arrival, "I'm no longer chief. Pradhan has disgraced me, and I've lost my position because of his despicable action. Can you help?"

Manjli's father looked up from the mat on which he sat inside the *manjhithan*. "Of course," he replied with confidence. "Who's your new chief?"

"Manu, at present. There's division in the village, but by luck, we can swing the vote."

"How does Manu feel about Christians?"

"Antagonistic."

"Good. That's encouraging. Now we must get Manu to call a council on Pradhan. Demand that both husband and wife come so we'll have a chance to face them together."

"My brother's becoming a Christian has complicated matters," Raghu confided. "They're sheltering Pradhan and his family."

"Dulu?"

The former chief nodded, even while rolling a pinch of

tobacco into a cigarette. Manjli's father watched, then accepted Raghu's offer, and rolled one for himself. The two men thought long thoughts while smoking. Finally Raghu's guest asked, "Can't you order Dulu to throw the family out? He's younger than you."

"No, for several reasons," Raghu responded. He rose, turned and pointed to the house on the adjoining compound. "See that house?" he asked. "That belongs to Dulu. If it belonged to me, I could take action."

"Hmmm . . . that does complicate matters."

"Moreover, my brother owns his land outside the village. He's independent enough to care for himself and my son."

Manjli's father drew a couple puffs on his cigarette, then suggested, "Under the circumstances, I think council pressure is the best route. Oh, I know. . . ." He slapped his knee with his free hand and exclaimed, "We'll bait Pradhan with becoming chief. Actually, that's his rightful position. And we'll threaten his wife unless he recants."

"You can try it," Raghu commented slowly, "but I don't believe my son is tempted by the position. He is extremely fond of Manjli. That's worth trying."

When Manu called the council to meet early Sunday morning, Dulu looked at Pradhan in dismay. "What's cooking, buddy?" he asked.

The younger man grinned, then said, "Plain as the nose on your face, man. Our parents are lying low, but they're behind this. I really expected it before. However, Sunday suits Dad's purposes better."

Dulu chuckled, "I get it. With the Christians in worship service, the rest can outvote us?"

"Right on, Andy!"

"Well, Steve, for this purpose, I'm very much Dulu, and I refuse giving my place on the council to someone else." He grinned then added, "You don't mind my missing worship?"

"Not when Manjli and I are on trial!"

"How do you know your parents are behind this?"

"Manu let it out. He said both Manjli and I are to be there, by order of our parents." .

"Whew! So we have a full-scale interrogation coming? All right. I'll pass the word along. Maya can take the children to the mission and request prayer for all of us."

"Bless you, Dulu. You never let me down!" He had hardly spoken when the drum beats began calling the council members together.

Kailu, Dukua, and Kailash got wind of the matter in time to join the council. Several other sympathizers also came. Raghu and his wife, sitting off to one side of the *manjhithan* with Manjli's parents, looked in dismay at the group that had gathered. He worried that getting an opposition vote might be a bigger problem that he anticipated.

"Stand in the middle," Manu ordered Pradhan and Manjli. It was a task not to his liking, his first official action as interim chief. From morning until noon the villagers pressed the young couple to recant.

Manjli's father opened the session by declaring, "Now that your father has stepped down from being chief, Pradhan, you are the rightful leader. He has trained you for this, and I understand you have a good record. Your very name declares this as his choice for you. For the sake of your people, let this foolhardy obsession go."

"If you are speaking about my following Jesus Christ, the answer is no!" the young man replied. "I'm not following a religion. I'm serving the living God! I've found Thakur Jiu, and I am more Santal now than I've ever been."

His father-in-law raged, "Manjli, listen to him! He's mad . . . out of his mind! How can he call a foreign god Thakur Jiu? This man's not a Santal. He's a traitor! Reject him. He's not fit to be your husband."

A quick glance passed between Manjli and Pradhan. She turned to her parents and answered softly, "I won't leave him."

That simply began the ordeal that continued for several hours. No amount of persuasion moved the young couple to recant. During this time of haranguing, Dulu and the other sympathizers kept quiet, but prayed fervently.

At noon, after futile efforts to resolve the matter, Manu

spoke. "Pradhan," he said, "this is your last chance. Do you renounce Christianity? If so, then you are chief. If not, we'll confiscate your possessions."

Dulu spoke swiftly, "No! I object! Manu, as a Santal, you can't do that. Pradhan is a member of my household. I'm living on my own land, doing my own farming. You have no legal hold on this couple. Their parents cast them out. As next of kin, we embraced them. They belong to us! Nor can you force them to decide in favor of your wishes. They're adults, with the freedom of choice. You may not touch their possessions, for they're members of my family."

"He speaks the truth! What he says is true!" Kailu and the sympathizers reiterated. "Remember the council decision on Jatha," they warned.

Raghu sat mute, a disappointed man. His wife took up the cause. She began to plead, "Say something, son. Give it up. You will be chief, you know."

"Sorry, mother. I have found true inner peace in Jesus. I can never renounce him or leave him. Do what you like to me, but know this, I will be a Christian."

"Your curses have fallen on our head," she sobbed. "You say you love your father, but look at what you've done to him."

Pradhan's chin quavered, and his eyes were filled with pain, yet he said quietly, "I would that not only I, but that all of you here would realize how much the Lord Jesus Christ has suffered for us . . . even to death. Can I do less for him?"

Manjli's father spoke angrily, "It's enough, daughter. You must leave this mad man and come home with us. We'll arrange another marriage for you."

A quick glance of love and understanding passed between the young couple. Pradhan dared to look at Dulu for a brief moment while Manjli answered, "No, Papa. I choose Pradhan."

Her mother spoke, "How can you, Manjli?" The woman's voice sounded like a sob, and Pradhan's mother tried once again, "Son, they're taking away your wife! Give it up for the sake of your aging parents and family."

Pradhan darted Dulu another glance, one that strengthened his resolve to stand. He stood tall and straight and answered, "I have given my final word. I will not leave Jesus Christ, regardless of cost."

"I refuse to go with my parents," Manjli announced firmly. "I stand with my husband."

"But you'll have no part in our inheritance! We won't perform your burial ceremony, or your final feast." It was their ultimate threat.

Raghu's son smiled and reiterated, "Do whatever you like with either Manjli or me. I will not recant."

"Let them alone," the sympathizers said, and the others, now weary from the battle, agreed.

Dukua spoke up. "We are witnesses. Pradhan has chosen, and I vote to make Manu our new chief."

That vote placed Manu into the position he had sought, but one that he obtained only to find it bitter in his mouth.

Chapter Seventeen

Persecution and Pakku

With the council now history, Manjli's parents left on Monday for home, and life in Raghu's courtyard became more or less normal. Tempers cooled, and the empty house next to the chief's home served as a reminder of a son gone. Raghu's lost status as chief also made the man bitter. His wife decided to push for Salku's wedding to give Raghu a new interest in life.

They found a young girl from Jhungi village. Very soon the courtyard resounded again, but this time with the singing of the women, and the throaty cries of men who had drunk to the point of inebriety.

Not one Christian was invited! Not even Dulu or Pradhan! But they learned of it in a rather unexpected manner.

One day Manjli darted around the house to the back courtyard where Maya sat cleaning vegetables. "Guess what?" she said breathlessly. "Puchu talked to me this morning."

"He did? What did he say?"

"That Salku's wedding is going to take place tomorrow. Isn't it strange they haven't said anything to us about it?"

Maya looked at the eager young woman with a smile, then answered, "Not strange at all. Manjli, dear, Pradhan's parents don't count him any more as a member of the family—and perhaps, since we took you in, we're also outcasts."

"Oh, I see!" The distraught girl threw herself at the older woman's feet.

"What's the matter?"

"I . . . we . . . we're causing you so much trouble!"

Maya touched her lovingly, then lifted her up. "No, Manjli, you must never say so again," she said. "This is very little to pay for all that the Lord Jesus has done for us."

117

It was the first of many such lessons on rejection the two couples were to receive.

Though they began by eating and working together, with Pradhan accompanying Dulu to the fields, the Pastor shook his head and soon offered some wise advice. "Regardless of how much you love each other," he began with a twinkle and a nod, "I suggest you cook separately, and as soon as possible, get under two roofs."

"Why, Benjamin?" Dulu asked after the regular music session had concluded.

"Well, if you do it from the beginning, the opposition won't have a chance to accuse you if later you decide to separate."

"But we enjoy being together," Dulu remonstrated.

"That's good," the white-haired preacher said with a nod. "This is of necessity, and you have done a very fine Christian thing by opening your home, Andrew. But I still say no roof is big enough to hold two families."

"But we are one, Benjamin," Pradhan argued. Yet within his heart he knew the Pastor had spoken well, so he added, "I believe you're right, and I think I see what you mean."

"Yes?"

"It's better to separate before we have differences. Is that it?"

"Very good, my sons. Share your compound, and show the community you're not running away. Build a nice house as soon as you can, Stephen. Yes, it is good. . . . "

"Thank you, Benjamin," Dulu said quietly. "I don't see any interference in the future, but I know you've lived longer than we have."

This talk resulted in Pradhan and Manjli doing their own housekeeping, however simple it was. The girl built a stove near their corner of the house, and in fun they'd "invite" their neighbors to share some delicacy. It set a pattern for each family retaining its own independence, something that worked for the good of all. Yet they exhibited a beautiful love for one another that brought them together in the early mornings and evenings to sing and worship and praise.

Pradhan sought a job doing road work. That, too, came as a result of Benjamin's advice. It also answered a big concern expressed by Dulu one day as they sat talking on the verandah to the patter of the midwinter rains.

"Buddy," he began, "I'm glad to share my land, but it simply isn't large enough to maintain both families. As I see it, you need some other source of income."

Pradhan laughed and stretched, then replied, "As usual, you're right. I love farming, but I'm going to have to forget it. I think I'll ask that *dikku* for a job where the government is repairing roads between here and Barhara Kothi. That way I'd have steady work, yet I could get off when you need help in your fields, Dulu."

"You're sure you want to do day labor? The opposition will laugh at you."

"Perhaps so."

"And you'd have to work long hours. . . . "

"With high pay," the young man concluded with a grin.

Within several months Pradhan saved enough money to build himself a new house comparable to any around, with the additional feature of a window! The villagers marveled and said, "His God is taking care of him."

Yet, in those intervening months, Pradhan and Manjli were not without trouble. Indeed, they became the target for mischief. Vegetables disappeared from the small garden plot Dulu gave them. Raising anything became a problem for the new Christian couple.

In the two months following Salku's wedding, Manjli kept watching for his bride, and managed to spot her once or twice. She's got a sweet face, she decided, but she's so young. I'd like to meet her.

A day or two later Manjli walked over to the other house, with her baby on her hip. "Maya, Maya," she called.

"I'm here, Manjli," the woman answered from the back of the house, and the girl soon joined her. She placed Moses on the ground, then said with a giggle, "You'll never believe what happened, Maya!" The baby started investigating everything around the tree, for his newly-acquired walking skills intrigued him.

"What is it?" Maya asked.

"Here, let me help. . . . " Manjli sat on the mat, picked up some beans and began cleaning them, then placed them in the vessel at her companion's side. "Guess what?" she reiterated. "Remember I told you someone stole our vegetables again from our garden?"

"Yes, I recall. What now?"

"You know . . . it's been hard, especially last week. We scarcely had enough to eat until Pradhan got his pay."

"Manjli! You should have told me!"

"No, Maya, don't feel sorry for us. Pradhan and I decided we're going to trust the Lord. You've already done so much for us . . . but just listen to this! Would you believe it? I just met Pakku, Salku's bride!"

"You did? Where?"

"Right behind our house there's a corner that isn't visible from the road. Pakku came there, and called me! She's smart! And you'll never believe what she brought. . . . "

"Yes?" Maya laid her knife and beans down and looked directly into the girl's animated features.

"A whole bunch of fresh vegetables!" she whispered.

"Hmmm . . . that's interesting," Maya said with a thoughtful look. "What do you make of it?"

"I think Salku stole our vegetables, and Pakku found out. So she's trying to make it up to me."

"Maybe so, although I wouldn't blame Salku without evidence. Plenty others in this village would gladly do the same, just to make things harder for you." The woman began working with her beans again, then asked, "What's Pakku like?"

"She's young, about thirteen or fourteen, I'd say. She has a round, open face and a puckish smile. And she says she likes Christians, Maya!"

Dulu's wife said thoughtfully, "Could it be possible she's a believer? It's very unusual for a girl to be so adventurous in such a household."

"She said everybody had gone to market. Maya, how can I find out if she's a believer?"

"We'll pray about it together. Since the Lord brought her once, he can bring her again."

When Manjli told Pradhan about the incident, he quietly suggested to Dulu to cut the fence at that location, and put in a turnstile. That evening they worked in the twilight and put in a small swinging gate.

For several days all remained quiet, then in midafternoon on market day Manjli heard a voice underneath her window. "Yes?" she answered. "Who is it?"

"Pakku, Manjli."

"Come in quickly," she exclaimed and opened the door. Salku's bride slipped in. With a toss of her head and a puckish grin she announced, "She's gone to market! I thought she'd take me as usual, but today Ma told me to stay home and grind grain. I just finished it," the girl said, giggling. "So I came over."

"Bless you," Manjli said, giving Pakku a hug. "Did you use the new gate?"

"Of course! All of you put it there for me, didn't you?"

"What will Salku say?"

"They're going to get it back on you . . . they're going to use that new gate tonight to come in and steal Pradhan's goat." She paused, then added, "I thought you ought to know . . . and they plan to use the meat for a feast to the *bongas* tomorrow. I think that's terrible!"

"Well, the Lord can take care of us without the goat meat. He sent you with vegetables, just at the right time. Believe me, we really enjoyed them, Pakku. Thank you, my dear!" She hugged the girl again.

Tears glistened in the younger girl's eyes. She said with a toss of her head, "We didn't need those, and you have to eat. Don't you mind people stealing your goat?"

"It hurts, of course, but we're ready to suffer for Jesus' sake." Manjli placed her hands on Pakku's shoulders and asked, "I've been wondering. Do you believe in Jesus?"

The tears spilled over. Wiping them with her cotton shawl, the girl whispered, "Yes, Manjli. I love him, and that's why I loved you as soon as I saw you."

"But where did you hear about him?"

"In Jhungi, my village. A leper family there became Christians. Every time the white-haired preacher visited, I joined the crowds. I love his music and stories, and I've stopped worshiping the *bongas*."

"I wish you could attend our meetings in the schoolhouse, Pakku."

"I thought I'd be able to if I married someone from Khanua. But," she sighed, shaking her head, "not with things as they are next door."

"Bless you, Pakku! Could you slip over sometimes to see Maya and me? We could pray together."

The girl laughed, and with a defiant toss of her head, she promised, "I'll come! You can count on me." She peeked out the window and said, "All quiet, still . . . but I should go."

"But let me pray with you, first," Manjli suggested.

Pakku managed to slip over about once a week. The two couples thrilled to know the Lord expected to continue the battle next door. Pakku's faith would prove a powerful wedge into the family resistance if she held true. But, to protect the girl, neither couple mentioned her spiritual openness to even Benjamin.

Almost a year had passed since Jatha had stepped out and taken baptism. One night, when Pradhan returned from the music class, he whispered to Manjli, "We're going to Banmankhi."

"For what?" she asked. "Come, let's talk on the verandah."

"It's Bible School," he replied. "Ten days to study the Bible! Oh, Manjli!"

She laughed, then said, "Yes, Pradhan, I'm ready. I'll request baptism."

"You and your intuition! How did you know what I wanted?"

"Nothing to it," she scoffed. "I can tell by looking at your face."

He chuckled, and drew her close, then said, "I'll have to ask for leave again, but the foreman's very considerate."

She leaned against his shoulder, then said, "Our money ran out last time—when you helped Dulu in his field work. Remember?"

"But the Lord sent Pakku," he reminded Manjli. "Let's see what he does this time."

Chapter Eighteen
Banmankhi Celebration

A mile south of the Banmankhi railway station, past the extensive Muslim village in which both Wolie the carpenter and Manku the gardener lived, the luxuriant mission compound became the wonder of the community.

Fifteen months previous, the American missionary family had moved into a grass-thatch house much like their neighbors'. However, this one had a cement floor.

People laughed when the mission bought farmed-out land, but not for long. Before their eyes they witnessed a transformation. Flowering shrubs and trees, nurtured by the Sahib who personally ordered over a hundred cartloads of fertilizer, replaced the former barrenness.

Manku watched it happen. His enthusiastic accounts made Sohan Lal and his friends curious. Soon the elite took their evening strolls to see the Sahib's garden.

"How did you do it, Sahib Ji?" they inquired.

"Come and see," he invited them. His "open door" policy warmed their hearts, and they concluded he was very different from the British government officials they had previously known. Even Sohan Lal had to admit to Wolie that the builder Sahib had transformed drabness into something beautiful.

Wolie, Manku, Bashir, and others who worked with the missionaries kept the town supplied with gossip. What were they teaching? The large Muslim village of Bishanpur, neighboring the mission, asked for a demonstration, and received a complete series of teaching on the life of Christ, the same material later used in Khanua.

But it was Santals, not Muslims, who responded to the gospel. New converts needed to be grounded in the Word of God, so Banmankhi mission became a retreat center, hosting not only Santals but many other groups through the succeeding years.

Within a year of arriving in Banmankhi, the missionary family moved into a modest three-room bungalow, fronted by a spacious verandah. This released "Alpha Cottage" to provide much needed dormitory space for hosting the new believers. The Sahib pitched a khaki tent for meetings, and several large tents for dormitories. Later, a quonset hut of aluminum served as chapel, and additional quonset huts became missionary quarters.

But no retreat could compare to that first Bible School session! The thrill of seeing a new church birthed, of recognizing each believer as a precious person won by Jesus Christ more than compensated for any trials. How many would come? The missionary family eagerly watched the road to the north.

Thirty people gathered at the mission compound in Khanua expecting to attend the Bible School sessions. Just before they started, however, a woman carrying an empty water pot arrived. She said quickly, "I hoped to catch you in time. The opposition expects to oust all of you when you've left the village."

Pastor Benjamin blinked rapidly, then asked, "Are you sure?"

"Yes, Pastor," she replied. "I overheard my husband and some of the others scheming last night. They said there's a strong enough majority in the village to override the Christian vote if they're not in the council."

"Hmmm . . ." Benjamin thought a moment, then announced, "I suggest one member of each household returns to maintain residence. What do you think?"

The group nodded approval, and the preacher suggested, "You may alternate, if you please. Everybody should have the chance to attend."

Dulu turned to Pradhan. "I'll stay this time," he said. "Maya wants to be baptized, so she must go. And buddy, I'd say my vote and presence will count for more than yours right now . . . right?"

"Right, Dulu! Look after our vegetables . . . and our goat!" he quipped with a grin.

Within ten minutes every household had decided on their course of action. Some divided the time so that each family member would have a chance to study the Bible. Others, like Dulu, decided the voting member should remain to protect the Christian community. All knew that the Lord had intercepted Satan's plan once again by alerting them to the danger.

Pradhan and Manjli with their sons, Joseph and Moses, met Patras and Sukul and their families with great joy. Over sixty new believers came together, converging from many villages now touched by the gospel.

They walked single file, men carrying loads on their shoulders, women bearing burdens on their heads. Maya held Joseph and Sam by the hand while Manjli carried the baby.

Their quiet procession through the Muslim village caused much comment from curious onlookers. But all marveled that so many had already turned to Christ.

Pradhan felt a growing excitement as he and Manjli neared the mission. On the outskirts of the Muslim village the road swerved left. It passed the Sahib's productive garden fronting the whitewashed bungalow and lawn. It followed the border of banana trees, continuing eastward to join another road to the main gate of the compound.

The group from Khanua hastened as they neared the gate. Waiting for them was their little white-faced *pakku*, in her arms her beautiful dollie, Shirley. Dina put her bundle down, swooped Joanne into her arms, and to the laughter of the entire group, carried her like a queen into Alpha Cottage. They were at home!

The ladies had no sooner settled into their dormitory quarters in Alpha Cottage until Manjli met a round-faced, starry-eyed Santal girl at the gate. Pakku, Salku's bride of three months, giggled.

Manjli cried in astonishment, "Pakku!" She rushed forward, and the two girls warmly embraced each other. "How did you get here?" she asked.

"Walked, of course."

"Silly," Manjli scolded. "You know what I mean. Where's Salku?"

"At the station, on his way to Purnea. I persuaded him to leave me with you instead of with his mother."

"What's he doing in Purnea?"

"His dad sent him on some land deal, I think. You want to

know something?" Pakku lowered her voice, then said, "He's beginning to listen to me. He used to lead his brothers in opposing Christians, but not now. . . ."

The girls had reached the front verandah of Alpha Cottage and the newcomer placed her bundle on the cement floor. Pakku faced Manjli and said, "I've prayed every day to come to Bible School!"

"What happened?"

"Since you and I have been praying together, I've had more courage to speak. You know, Manjli, Salku beat me twice, but the Lord helped me. So now he knows there's something to Christianity after all. He's been watching Pradhan and Dulu, too."

"And here we thought he was terribly opposed to us."

"You'd be surprised how many people are watching you! I hear them talk," the girl said.

"Wait until I tell Pradhan!"

Just then Maya and Dina walked into sight, so Pakku ran to meet them. Manjli turned back to pick up the baby, then rushed off to find her husband, and soon joined him for meeting.

Pradhan looked around the group gathered in the khaki tent. He thrilled to be able to read the Scriptures for himself, and he proudly opened the Santali New Testament he had bought. With the others he learned key Scriptures and new songs.

Everything was new! The Bible verses that the Memsahib taught by rote . . . the delightful Santal lyrics that Pastor Benjamin so patiently explained . . . the homespun messages he gave, and the doctrinal teaching the Sahib gave with Pastor interpreting from Hindi into Santali. But perhaps the most outstanding feature to Pradhan and the other new believers was the fellowship of those who like him had left *bonga* worship for the privilege of knowing Christ Jesus as Lord.

Joy characterized their testimonies. Time held little or no meaning. At that first institute, new believers learned they were part of the body of Christ, gifted by the Holy Spirit, their bodies his temple. And the wonder of it all held them spellbound.

Understandably, then, the new church grew within the framework of patience and love. That Bible School held many surprises. One, nobody could have anticipated!

Word reached Gopal Singh that fifteen villagers were attending meetings in Banmankhi. He fumed while his son listened.

"Ram Das," he exploded, "where will this end? I can't do anything because at least one family member has stayed in each house. They'd better take care of their field work, or else."

"So what, Dad? If all of them went to the bazaar, you wouldn't care a hoot! Why get fussed up if they go somewhere else?"

"What's wrong with you? I don't understand you these days."

"Well, my respected father, I've been making some inquiries on my own. If you'll permit, I'd like to walk down by the mission in Banmankhi on my way to Purnea tomorrow. I can check things out for you, if that's any satisfaction."

"Good idea, boy." Gopal Singh adjusted his turban, then rubbed his hands together and said, "Yes, bring me a report. If you need to stay an extra day, it's worth it to keep tab on those Christians."

The young man smiled slightly. He decided his dad wasn't at all hard to manipulate.

During the late afternoon of the following day, the young Brahman walked to the mission site. He passed by once, then returned to find Pastor Benjamin standing near the front gate. The white-haired preacher started in surprise. "Ram Das!" he exclaimed. "What brings you here?"

"Good day, Benjamin," the young man replied. "My father is sending me on business to Purnea, and I've taken the chance to see the mission. I heard the Sahib has done wonders with this farmed-out land. All of Banmankhi bazaar is talking about it." He gazed in admiration at the lush garden and flowers, then waved his arm and said, "It's nice, isn't it?"

The preacher wrinkled up his nose and wiped his glasses carefully. He wasn't yet sure of this young man's intent, yet he seemed harmless. The Brahman laughed curtly, "Don't fear," he said, "I'm not spying on you."

"Oh?" the preacher answered. "Then what?"

"Could we talk alone somewhere?"

A glance at the position of the sun assured Benjamin he had an hour to spare prior to service, so he suggested, "Let's walk in the bamboo grove to the south of the mission. There you can talk freely."

"Thank you," Ram Das said. He began, "Perhaps you didn't recognize me, but I listened to you every night but one—last year in Khanua."

"Is that so?" the preacher said in amazement.

"Yes," he said with a nod. "I came to ridicule, but your message got hold of me, Pastor. I've never been the same since."

"In what way?"

"I've studied the Bible in college, Pastor . . . as world literature, you know. But it didn't grip me the way your messages did when you explained the life of Christ to your people. Somehow, Jesus Christ became real to me, and I saw his perfection—and my sinfulness."

Benjamin Mirandy stopped and faced his companion. "Are you telling the truth?"

The young man laughed curtly. "Yes, sir, I am. I don't have much of a reputation for it, but I've never been more serious. I hope you can believe me."

Benjamin took off his glasses and wiped his eyes. Putting them back on, he said, "Forgive me for doubting you, Ram Das. Please continue."

"It's Christ's perfection that gets me. I can't find any lack in him, and that bothers me."

"Yes, I see," the preacher responded. "He is the God-Man, the perfect One. Because of that very perfection, he alone can be the sacrifice for our sins. Don't you see? Nobody else is good enough!"

The young man stopped short. "You remind me of something I've read in the Hindu scriptures."

"Oh?"

"Yes! In Sanskrit it says in Tandya Maha Brahmanam of Sama Veda, '*Prajapatir devebhyam atmanam yognam krutva prayachhat.*' "

The preacher blinked his eyes several times. Ram Das had introduced something completely foreign to him, so he asked, "What's that?"

"It says God will offer himself as a sacrifice and obtain atonement for sins," the excited young man replied.

"Is that so?" the white-haired preacher exclaimed. "Would you know I've offered so many chickens in sacrifice that I can prepare them at night with my own bare hands?"

"You did?"

"It never brought peace. Only when I believed in Jesus did I find forgiveness for sin and peace of heart. Ram Das, won't you come to him, too?"

"I'm not sure yet. I want to study the Bible for myself."

"You're going to Purnea?"

"Yes."

"Hunt up the missionary ladies there, and buy a Hindi Bible from them."

"Thank you, but first, I'd like to attend the meeting this evening. Do you think the Santals would mind?"

Benjamin blinked rapidly, then answered, "If I vouch for you, they'll accept you."

By prearrangement the preacher returned first to the mission compound, and the Brahman young man came in after the meeting had started. He sat in the back, listening again to the sweet message of Jesus and his love.

Like Ram Das, some sat through just one meeting, but went away impressed. Other observers found themselves involved to the extent of staying several days. And for such eager students as Pradhan and the group from Khanua, the ten days passed far too quickly. True, he missed Dulu, but knew that they could share together again on his return.

The meetings and crowd gained in strength as Easter approached. On Easter Sunday morning Manjli and Maya requested baptism. Pradhan's wife chose the name Sarah, and Maya became Mary.

Pradhan, with Joseph by his side, watched intently. Little Moses knew no inhibitions in that sacred moment. Held by Dina, he pointed and said, "Ma!" Everybody laughed. At the conclusion of the services a new Manjli came to her husband and said, "I'm Sarah, now, and you are Stephen."

Long after the women and children's voices stilled within their quarters, the men continued singing out under the light of a full moon. To the fine tones and half-tones of Benjamin's violin and the rhythmic beat of Daniel's cantone, their voices rose and fell in praise to God.

The white-haired preacher looked around and smiled. Where there had been no church a year ago, now forty men joined him in praise.

The tempo accelerated, and joy increased. One lyric followed another, bonding these new believers in a unity of spirit they had never before experienced. Stephen felt it surging within. His past dropped away, and he stood at the threshold of a new beginning. In that moment of true worship, as with one motion, the men stood, formed a circle and danced before the Lord. Their measured steps—backward, then forward, arms linked—reminded two spectators sitting in awe on the mission bungalow verandah of King David's dancing before the Lord. Wherein David had been truly Jew, expressing his love and adoration in terms familiar to him, these men now were truly Santal, yet truly Christian!

Tomorrow they would each return to the village, to live out in practical terms that which God had birthed within their hearts by the Holy Spirit.

Chapter Nineteen

The Chief and His Son

Eight years later, on a beautiful Sunday morning, Khanua village glistened in the sunlight. A recent shower had freshened the earth, and its fragrance wafted over the morning breeze.

The newly-arrived pastor of the neat brick church on the mission compound stepped onto the verandah of his home. His thoughts whirled back to another Sunday morning when he and his wife stood before a council in that same village. He could hear his mother's broken pleading, "Son, they're taking your wife! Give it up for the sake of your aging parents and family." He remembered his reply, "Mother, I have given my final word. I will not renounce Jesus Christ, regardless of cost." He felt again the emotion of that high moment when his beautiful Sarah, then Manjli, declared, "I refuse to accompany my parents. I stand with my husband."

Now, eight years later, in that same village, an embittered old man nursed his grief. Bereaved by the sudden death of his wife, Raghu had disowned Salku and Pakku when they took baptism. As Luke and Naomi, the young couple left the village and journeyed to Assam where they worked on tea plantations and spread the gospel among their own people.

When Raghu's younger sons told their father of Stephen's appointment to the pastorate of the mission church, he declared, "He's no son of mine! I forbid him to ever place foot within my house."

But Pastor Stephen kept hoping and praying. If the Lord could reunite Kailu and his estranged wife, if he could break Salku's antagonism and turn him into a Christian witness, dare the new pastor doubt a further miracle? Surely God would hear.

Stephen bowed his head once again and affirmed that the Lord would bring the former chief to himself.

Khanua seethed with excitement. Long before the second bell rang for church, Dulu and Maya, now Andrew and Mary, gathered with other villagers for the extended welcome they planned for the pastor on this, his first Sunday.

Much laughter gave way to singing and praise. True, the former witch doctor's violin was now missing. But Stephen played another. The audience followed its sweet cadences, tones, and mini-tones, in the hauntingly beautiful Santal lyrics. Then the new pastor preached. He scanned every face, rejoicing in those who were there, but missing the one he sought.

Each succeeding Sunday Stephen yearned over his people. Several weeks after his arrival, he answered a knock on his front door. It was Sunday morning, about time to ring the first bell for service.

"Ram Das!" Khanua's new pastor exclaimed. "Come in, come in."

"Thank you, Pastor, but I wondered whether we could talk over at the church?"

"Yes, yes . . . I was on my way to ring the first bell. Come with me." The men chatted as they walked to the neat red brick building with the cross on top.

"I wish I had your courage," Gopal Singh's son began.

"Why?"

"I've wanted to take baptism for years. I've been a secret believer ever since I moved to Purnea."

"I hadn't heard."

"Let's go back to the special council. Several months after that, you recall I stopped overnight in Banmankhi on my way to Purnea on business?"

Stephen nodded, then said, "I've been interested in you ever since, and I've prayed for you regularly."

"Outwardly I continued to perform the Hindu rites to satisfy my mother, but being with you Christians proved a turning point in my life. Pastor Benjamin told me about two missionary ladies in Purnea, and I bought a Hindi Bible from them. What I read convinced me of Christ's claims."

By this time the men had reached the church, and the pastor

said, "Excuse me until I ring the bell. Then we can continue." When Stephen returned, the men sat together on the front seat and the pastor inquired, "So you moved to Purnea, Ram Das?"

"Yes, my father opened a business and I managed the business for him until after I was married. In Purnea I began to listen to Christian radio programs."

"Oh? Which ones?"

"To *Vandana* (Worship Time) from Sri Lanka, and to the Hindi programs from FEBA Seychelles, you know." Ram Das smiled and pushed his heavy black hair off his forehead.

"Well," the pastor mused, "I'd say that evening service in Banmankhi bore far-reaching results. I'm glad."

"Your testimony helped too, Pradhan."

"Stephen, please."

"Yes—Stephen. We heard about your vegetable garden being raided and your goat stolen. We laughed with your persecutors when we learned you turned to road work to maintain yourself—you, a superb farmer! But I noticed you quickly became financially independent, and I liked your new house with a window. You see, I did watch you!"

Stephen grinned, but said nothing. "You taught me that none of us lives to ourself. We extend a shadow that falls on others."

"Why, thank you, friend. I'm greatly encouraged! As I said, I've prayed for you often, and I hope you will accept the Lord Jesus as your personal Savior." He paused, then added, "I miss Pastor Benjamin. It's a big place I'm supposed to fill!"

"Where is he?"

"Opening up another area. Well, I must get ready for service, but let me pray for you first. Will you stay for meeting?"

"Not today. My wife and children are with me on hot-weather leave."

After prayer Ram Das said, "One more thing, Stephen. I used to despise you, and I did you great harm. Please forgive me. If I ever step out publicly, it will be greatly because of your influence. Thank you."

Sunday after Sunday Stephen scanned his audience for the face of an embittered old man. Almost a year passed, but that desire persisted. He knew that his father sat in his house alone while his son poured out his heart in the little red brick church nearby. Surely the God of miracles would hear prayer and answer.

One memorable Sunday, the pastor recognized his father sitting at the back, white cotton sheet pulled securely around him. His heart leaped in hope!

That day his message poured forth in torrents, a passionate portrayal of God's love and forgiveness through Jesus Christ. A hush settled over the congregation. Several stood to confess their backslidings and others made new commitments. But the old man withdrew before the conclusion of the service, and his son sensed deep dismay. Yet Stephen knew his father had listened to the gospel. The Spirit of God would do the rest.

However, Raghu awaited his son on the verandah of the parsonage. His dimmed eyes took on new light as he watched the family approaching.

"Sarah! It's my father!" Stephen whispered. "I think he wants to see me alone. Take the boys and go around the back way. I'll try to persuade him to stay and eat with us."

She nodded and took Tabitha by the hand. "Joseph and Moses," she called to the two boys who skipped ahead, "come this way."

Stephen hastened toward the man sitting on his haunches, cotton sheet pulled around thin shoulders. "Father!" he exclaimed. Raghu looked up, then stood.

"I've come, Pradhan," he said brokenly.

"It's been a long time, but I kept hoping and praying."

"I wanted to hear you preach. Others gave good reports of you."

The former chief bowed his head, then lifted it to look deep into Stephen's gleaming eyes. He said slowly, "If you can forgive an old man's folly, I ask you to forgive me. And . . . I invite you home, whenever you care to come."

Stephen could only nod. Raghu continued, "The village respects your leadership, son. I want you to know I'm proud of you."

Stephen bowed low. Voice choked with emotion, he whispered, "Bless me once more, father."

The former chief raised his right hand in ceremonial blessing and murmured, "You have blessed me, Pradhan. You brought me the Light."

The young man's two strong arms suddenly enfolded that withered frame as within the old man's cold heart a new warmth gushed forth, an elixir of joy. As in a daze, he heard the invitation, "Come, my father. Dinner is ready. We've been waiting for you."

About the author

Leoda Buckwalter, daughter of missionary parents, calls India home. Her first eleven years as a child, followed by forty years of service as a missionary with her husband Allen (1939-1981), give her an intimate knowledge of the land of her birth. She is familiar with both rural India and urban India, having lived two decades in each as an adult.

With such a background, the author comes to us with her second book. *Silhouette,* released in 1988, catches the reader with oft-times humorous and down-to-earth experiences of the Buckwalters through the war years (1939-47). *The Chief's Son* focuses on the fascinating six-year adventure of living and working among a tribal group, the Santals. Both books are published by Evangel Press.